What people are s

Healing Social

I consider Barry Spivack's work very important.
Maeve Cooke, Professor of Philosophy, University College Dublin, and author of *Re-Presenting the Good Society*

For anyone vexed by the problem of conflict and hatred, this book has good news. *Healing Social Divisions* offers a line of intervention that is relatively straightforward: meditation can heal social divisions even if only a small fraction of people practise it. Analysing the effectiveness of meditation interventions is challenging but the book does a great job to explain social behaviour. I enjoyed reading the book, as it is easy to follow and truly entertaining.
Bernhard Reinsberg, Lecturer in International Relations, Glasgow University

Healing Social Divisions opens our eyes to a welcome and urgently needed new possibility for humankind. It provides a vision both sweepingly grand and immediately practical.
Bob Roth, CEO of the David Lynch Foundation and author of the best-selling book *Strength in Stillness*

Conflict and hatred have real economic costs in addition to reducing individual and collective well being. In this book, Barry Spivack lays out both the theoretical foundations and empirical evidence for the practice of Transcendental Meditation in healing social divisions and reducing conflict and hatred in society. This is a very timely book and one that should inspire policy makers across the globe.
Huw Dixon, Professor of Economics, Cardiff University

Barry Spivack's book is well grounded in this work and ventures further, exploring the body of research that suggests groups of meditators can positively affect the wellbeing of societies.
Miguel Farias, DPhil, co-author of *The Buddha Pill: Can Meditation Change You?* and lead editor of the *Oxford Handbook of Meditation*

Healing Social Divisions

The truth of life, liberty and the pursuit of happiness

Healing Social Divisions

The truth of life, liberty and
the pursuit of happiness

Barry Spivack

CHANGEMAKERS
BOOKS

Winchester, UK
Washington, USA

JOHN HUNT PUBLISHING

First published by Changemakers Books, 2022
Changemakers Books is an imprint of John Hunt Publishing Ltd., No. 3 East Street,
Alresford, Hampshire SO24 9EE, UK
office@jhpbooks.com
www.johnhuntpublishing.com
www.changemakers-books.com

For distributor details and how to order please visit the 'Ordering' section on our website.

Text copyright: Barry Spivack 2021

ISBN: 978 1 78535 969 9
978 1 78535 970 5 (ebook)
Library of Congress Control Number: 2021942748

A CIP catalogue record for this book is available from the British Library.

Design: Matthew Greenfield

UK: Printed and bound by CPI Group (UK) Ltd, Croydon, CR0 4YY
Printed in North America by CPI GPS partners

We operate a distinctive and ethical publishing philosophy in
all areas of our business, from our global network of authors to
production and worldwide distribution.

Contents

Preface and acknowledgements

When the book I co-authored with Dr Patricia Saunders, *An Antidote to Violence: Evaluating the Evidence*, was published in the summer of 2020, I had no thoughts of writing a second. However, it wasn't long before ideas for titles started to pass through my mind: *government and collective consciousness; truth, freedom and happiness; after Brexit, Trump and Covid*, and variations around those themes. In November 2020 I began writing *Healing Social Divisions*.

An Antidote to Violence examines peer-reviewed research which provides evidence that creating more coherence or orderliness in the collective consciousness of a society could reduce violence. In particular we wanted to explore how well this research could stand up to potential and actual criticisms. In the social sciences it is difficult to show cause and effect, but we concluded that there were sufficient good-quality studies, compared with normal standards in the social sciences, to justify governments undertaking their own research, and in some countries this is beginning to happen.

An Antidote to Violence focuses on empirical research; it does not emphasize the implications for freedom, happiness and social harmony. While the previous book examines the concept of collective consciousness, it does not analyse in detail what it is about the nature of human consciousness that has this potential to heal social divisions. A reduction in violence and an increase in social harmony are good things, but what then? This book, which is half the length of the other, covers a wide range of ideas and research studies indicating that we have the means to create a more creative and fulfilling society which can harmonize both unity and diversity.

I would particularly like to thank Patricia for finding the publisher, Changemakers Books; it made publication a much simpler process second time round. A big thank you to my first two readers, Kay Capes and Roberta Keenan, who read a draft almost twice the length of the finished version. Tim Ward, the publisher of Changemaker Books, can take a great deal of credit for reducing the word count, plus sharpening and clarifying the narrative. Special thanks to Bernard and Jane Bence. Thanks are due to Michael Dillbeck, John Hagelin, Peter Warburton, David Scharf, Gerry Geer and especially Volker Schanbacher. Also appreciation is owed to Steve Cross and Bernhard Reinsberg for their thoughtful comments. I am grateful for the feedback and help I received from Maeve Cooke, Ken Smith, Fred Travis, Ken Cavanaugh, David Orme-Johnson, Kingsley Brooks, Diane Scott, Joseph Zander, Phil Pearce, Neil Williamson, Louise McGuire, Glen McCoy, Sheila Chalmers and Robert Johnstone who all made useful contributions. Thanks to John Fuller for the illustrations in the book. A particular thank you to David Williams for his help with the cover. The staff at John Hunt Publishing made the process of production straightforward, especially Charlotte Edwards. If there is anything of value in the book, credit should go to Maharishi Mahesh Yogi; and for any errors, I have to take responsibility. And finally, thank you for reading this book.

Introduction

With about 200 states, 2,000 nations with claims on sacred space and with memories of sacred time and about 20 nation-states, there is a world potential for 1,980 independence wars, pitting status quo-orientated states against change-oriented nations.
John Galtung, *Searching for Peace*

When asked, in a very revealing survey, if there are parts of neighbouring countries that really belong to them, 67 per cent of Hungarians and 60 per cent of Greeks confirmed their ambitions to add to their existing territory, as did 58 per cent of Turkish citizens. Around half the population of Poland (48 per cent), Slovakia (46 per cent) and Bulgaria (58 per cent) also supported their country's right to territorial expansion...an equally depressing story can be told of mutual suspicions breeding division and disunity across both Africa and Asia.
Gordon Brown, *Seven Ways to Change the World*

After Joe Biden won the election to become President of the United States, he said:

I pledge to be a president who seeks not to divide, but to unify; who doesn't see red and blue states, but a United States...The Bible tells us that to everything there is a season – a time to build, a time to reap, a time to sow, and a time to heal. This is the time to heal in America.[1]

We live at a time when people cannot even agree on what is factual, so what hope is there to heal social divisions? I will outline a non-ideological method to heal social and international divides: if it were ideological it would create new divisions. Some may say a non-ideological approach to healing

1

disagreements is impossible and incoherent in principle; I hope to show otherwise.

An implication of Brexit and the 2016 election of Donald Trump as President of the USA is that in both countries there were large numbers of people whose views were not being represented by the established parties. These divides go back decades and the UK and US governments failed to maintain balance between diverse regions and different groups that make up these nations. The two nationalistic campaign slogans, *Take back control* and *Make America great again*, resonated with the respective electorates. These types of campaigns have the potential to light the fuse of social conflict. John Galtung is the principal founder of the discipline of peace studies, and the quote above suggests such latent divisions are never too far from tipping into civil unrest.[2] The aim of *Healing Social Divisions* is to explain an effective non-coercive method for preventing and resolving these differences before they lead to violence.

Ignoring concerns of a nation's citizens leads to a distrust of elites. During the 2020 pandemic we have witnessed scepticism towards political and scientific leaders, even though science and technology are the basis of much of what we take for granted in modern life. This has given rise to conspiracy theories and questions about sources of valid knowledge. History has many examples of real conspiracies, so it is not as if conspiracies do not happen. But because tobacco companies hid the fact that they knew about the risk of developing lung cancer as a result of regular smoking, it does not mean that there was never a moon landing. The flagrant abuse of truth during Brexit and the 2016 US presidential election was a motivating factor in writing *Healing Social Divisions*, and the issue of truth in public life will be touched on near the end.

Chapter 1 explains the key concept of neutralizing stress and increasing coherence in collective consciousness.[3] The following chapter further clarifies this consciousness-based approach to healing social divisions. Taking inspiration from the American Declaration of Independence, chapters 3, 4 and 5 investigate the peer-reviewed evidence that the quality of collective consciousness influences life, liberty and the pursuit of happiness. Chapter 3 gives ten reasons why decreases in violence and crime and increases in cooperation, which are correlated with greater coherence in collective consciousness, are consistent with a causal hypothesis. Chapter 6 explains why opposite qualities and social attitudes can be harmonized without external compulsion. Next I look at the relationship between collective consciousness and good governance and the way a government can harmonize conflicting values within a society and between nations. Chapter 7 outlines 12 principles of good governance. Good governance depends on choices, and choices are based on human consciousness. In a globalized world, good governance extends beyond national boundaries and depends on international cooperation, which is influenced by the amount of harmony in collective consciousness. The penultimate chapter explicitly challenges the conventional wisdom that consciousness is only a by-product of the functioning of the brain; rather it encourages a new scientific paradigm of an expanded understanding of human consciousness which is intimately connected with the values of freedom, happiness, harmony and truth. Finally I discuss how these proposals reduce narrowness of vision, enlarge our moral circle and may enhance higher standards in public life. An alternative title could be *Care of the Self and Political Change* as this book's theme is how progress and social and political cooperation depend on individual development.

How much of what we assume is correct will be laughed at in 200 years' time? This is especially true when it comes to governing as there is no consensus about the best way to run modern societies. *Healing Social Divisions* offers a new approach to good governance which may appear to be at odds with conventional forms of politics and political activism, but a closer inspection will show that it adds a new layer of understanding without diminishing existing approaches to improving society.

Chapter 1

Neutralizing social tensions

The totality of beliefs and sentiments common to the average members
of a society forms a determinate system with a life of its own.
Emile Durkheim, *The Division of Labour in Society*

James Carville, one of President Bill Clinton's strategists in
his successful 1992 presidential campaign, is credited with
the slogan *It's the economy, stupid*. Even though conservatives,
liberals and Marxists have contrasting views on how a country
should be organized, they all see the economy as a crucial driver
of society; economic materialism is seen as more fundamental
to social change than human consciousness. By contrast, Emile
Durkheim (1858–1917), one of the founding fathers of scientific
sociology, gave more emphasis to morality than to economics.

A unique aspect of Durkheim's thought was the idea of the
collective consciousness, which is more than the sum of the
parts of individual consciousnesses and has a life of its own. We
notice this when we travel from one country to another, France
to Germany, or from one region to another, New York City to
the Midwest. More rigorous evidence is to be found in Robert
Putnam's prize-winning study of the differences between north
and south Italy.[1] There can be a difference in the atmosphere, in
the norms and habits; and these norms can influence behaviour.

Durkheim makes a comparison with tin and copper, which
are both soft and malleable but when combined make bronze,
which is found to be hard; the whole is more than the sum of
the parts.

Just as the living cell is something other than the simple sum
of inanimate molecules constituting it, just as the organism

5

itself is something other than a sum of its cells, so is society a psychic being that has its own particular way of thought, feeling and action, differing from that peculiar to the individuals who compose it.[2]

Durkheim explained the collective consciousness in terms of shared norms and values that hold a society together and he called these social facts. Durkheim is known for his work on the different rates of suicide among Catholics and Protestants. "A social fact like suicide or collective consciousness", writes Durkheim expert Dr Kenneth Smith, "cannot live without us and yet is also not identical with us."[3]

In 1894 Durkheim's theory received a jolt from reality in the form of the Dreyfus affair. Alfred Dreyfus (1859–1935), a Jewish officer in the French army, was falsely accused of treason and subsequently imprisoned. As the son, grandson and great-grandson of rabbis, Durkheim "could not remain unaffected" as this legal case exposed the deep divisions existing in French society.[4] Smith suggests that as a result of the Dreyfus affair, Durkheim realized that the collective consciousness "might develop in an entirely aberrant way" and that the solution was for teachers and schools to instil the appropriate morality into impressionable children.[5] Durkheim, who became Professor of Education at the Sorbonne in Paris, had regarded the collective consciousness as something that occurred organically in a society, but after the Dreyfus affair his view changed; it was about educating children in the appropriate social norms. These are the unwritten rules of beliefs, attitudes, and behaviours that are considered acceptable in a particular social group or culture.

The premise of *Healing Social Divisions* is that governmental actions are a function of collective consciousness, and while there are some similarities to Durkheim, I will give a different explanation of the concept. This view of collective consciousness is taken from Maharishi Mahesh Yogi (1917–2008), an expert in the development of both individual and collective consciousness and the founder of the Transcendental Meditation organization.

1. The collective consciousness of a nation is made up from all the individuals. The different groups in which we all participate, including family, ethnic, religious, regional, race, national, occupational, and so on, will have their own flavour of collective consciousness.

2. The quality of collective consciousness can be more or less harmonious, orderly or coherent. Sometimes large crowds can be very orderly – think of a joyous national celebration – and sometimes a crowd can turn into an unruly mob.

3. There is a reciprocal relationship between the individual and society. The individual influences the collective consciousness and vice versa.

4. The unit of collective consciousness is the consciousness of the individual. It is through the individual consciousness alone that the collective consciousness becomes more coherent, orderly or harmonious.

5. Every government, regardless of its system, is an innocent mirror of the nation; government is not an independent entity. "Whatever is the quality of the collective consciousness of the nation," writes Maharishi, "that only can be the quality of its government."[6] And elsewhere he comments: "Although the members of every government have their own individuality and their own opinions of the nation's needs, while engaged in the process of governing, their actions are determined by factors beyond their personal lives – by the collective destiny of the nation."[7]

6. Rather than transforming the life of human beings and society from the outside by changing economic

structures and relations, Maharishi wanted to change human beings and society from the inside by enabling people to unfold their full potential. Like Durkheim, Maharishi placed an extremely high value on education, but his emphasis was on change coming from within rather than from outside, although both have their value.

7. In 1962 Maharishi suggested that even a relatively small proportion of a population practising the Transcendental Meditation technique would lead to measurable social changes, such as decreases in violence and increases in social harmony. This would begin to influence social trends in a measurable way and the greater the numbers, the bigger the effect.

As it was Maharishi who first predicted the improved quality of life due to practice of Transcendental Meditation, the phenomenon is known as the Maharishi Effect. The number of people practising Transcendental Meditation required to produce an influence will depend on the amount of stress and tension in society. Maharishi recommended having a safety factor of larger numbers to magnify the benefits, but the principle can be tested on a smaller scale. In Chapter 3, I will provide peer-reviewed evidence for the influence of collective consciousness in improving social trends. For decades, consciousness has been regarded as merely an epiphenomenon of the brain, but more recently this and other research has challenged that view.

It is the testability of the Maharishi Effect that distinguishes the idea of collective consciousness from similar-sounding ideas such as the collective unconscious, an idea developed by the Swiss psychiatrist and psychoanalyst Carl Jung (1875–1961). According to Jung, the collective unconscious is made up of a collection of knowledge and imagery that we are born with and is shared by all of us. Though we may not know what thoughts and images are in our collective unconscious, the idea is that in times of crisis we can tap into the collective unconscious. According to Jung the collective unconscious is expressed through universal concepts called archetypes. Archetypes may be signs, symbols, or patterns of thinking and behaving that are derived from our forebears. The problem with Jung's idea of the collective unconscious is that it is difficult to operationalize or test it by measurement. The question *Healing Social Divisions* answers is whether individual change through meditation can reduce an atmosphere of tension and hostility for the individual and society.

Pulling the arrow back on the bow

What distinguishes Transcendental Meditation from other meditations is the experience of transcendental consciousness. The meditator transcends, or goes beyond, the process of meditation and experiences consciousness on its own without an object of perception. We do not try to transcend; we just use a specific technique which allows the mind to spontaneously and effortlessly settle down by using the natural tendency of the mind to move in the direction of greater happiness. "One must not exert oneself in order to transcend," says Maharishi. "Exertion of any kind only retards the process of transcending."[8]

Any person, whatever their ethnic background, age, gender, religion or culture, can learn Transcendental Meditation. One doesn't have to believe in it to obtain the benefits: it is a mechanical technique. It requires no change in beliefs and no adoption of any new lifestyle or diet. In fact Maharishi places great emphasis on people following their own cultural traditions. All that is required is regular and effortless practice for 20 minutes, morning and evening, plus normal unstrained activity. And Transcendental Meditation has been successfully practised by people all over the globe.

Maharishi has commented: "The nervous system becomes more stable even under stressful stimuli. What we notice from this is that we seem to have our feet more on the ground. We are finding stability. We are finding more contentment within ourselves."[9]

It is like the process of pulling an arrow back on a bow until it is at a point of stillness and then one lets go. Similarly, mental activity is effortlessly brought to a state of quietness, and after meditation action is performed without strain and therefore is more effective. It is the experience of the simplest state of consciousness which preserves conscious inner awareness by itself, with minimum mental and physiological activity. Transcendental Meditation produces an influence of balance and orderliness in the brain and nervous system. The brainwave coherence and synchrony in the pre-frontal cortex in the alpha 1, 8–10 cycles per second frequency is unique to Transcendental Meditation and distinguishes it objectively from meditations involving either focused attention (concentration) or open monitoring (contemplation). In addition the default mode network, a large-scale network in the brain, is activated during Transcendental Meditation but is inhibited during other methods of meditation.[10]

Transcendental Meditation is derived from the Vedic tradition (Veda means knowledge) of India and Maharishi always gives all credit to his teacher Swami Brahmananda Saraswati. One may ask: why are there divisions and suffering in India? Maharishi explains:

There is a lot of talk of meditation, and many people practice one technique or another, but the whole field is one of confusion. The idea is there, but the simplicity has been lost. Evolution is natural to life, but people in India began using effort and concentration and it all became tedious and unnatural. The whole understanding about spiritual development was lost...These people are sold out to austerity. They think nothing can be gained without austerity, but they are mistaken. Struggle does not belong to the nature of life. One has to struggle only when he does not know how to grow without struggle...they say that desires should be cut down...It is not necessary to have any sense of detachment or renunciation, to abstain from life, to ignore the responsibilities of life.[11]

Instead of transcending, the emphasis in India had been on either concentration or contemplation. Maharishi writes: "If the occupants of a house forget the foundations, it is because the foundations lie underground, hidden from view. It is not a surprise that Being [transcendental consciousness] was lost to view, for It lies in the transcendental field of life."[12]

Claims of benefits are based on peer-reviewed evidence

Galileo didn't merely deny that the tides were caused by the Moon – he went as far as to mock Kepler's assertion that they do.
Maria Popova, *Figuring*

There have been more than 400 peer-reviewed studies on Transcendental Meditation and its advanced programmes.[13] We can divide these studies in two: those that measure physiological changes during meditation such as, for example, reductions in cortisol and plasma lactate; increases in the urinary metabolite of serotonin, arginine vasopressin, blood flow to the brain, and in integrated brain functioning as measured by an electroencephalograph (EEG); and those that measure changes outside of meditation such as increased creativity, reduced anxiety, improved health and better social behaviour both for the individual and society, including decreased violence. The research can be summarized as indicating the development of more balance and orderliness, which provides the platform for reduced suffering, greater progress and happiness in life.

This research has been carried out at more than 250 universities and research institutes in over 30 countries and published in more than 100 peer-reviewed journals. Two studies specifically investigated the question of experimenter allegiance and found that there was no significant difference between the results of studies, whether researchers were affiliated with the TM organization or were at an independent university.[14]

Archie Wilson, Professor of Medicine at the University of California at Irvine, did not practise Transcendental Meditation and he was involved with 20 studies on the physiological changes as a result of TM practice. Many of Wilson's subjects had been practising Transcendental Meditation for three to ten years which makes it unlikely the measured changes were due to the placebo effect as that is usually short-term. In recent years there have been more collaborative TM research projects involving more non-meditating scientists. Two examples are reductions in post-traumatic stress disorder (PTSD) in war veterans and reduced rates of reconviction in prison inmates who have learned Transcendental Meditation compared with control groups. These studies have been published in peer-reviewed journals such as *Lancet Psychiatry, Journal of Offender Rehabilitation, Criminal Justice and Behaviour, American Journal of Hypertension, Military Medicine*, and so on.

The first chart below shows a typical EEG tracing when a person is not meditating, which is a rapidly changing composite or combination of different brainwaves moving up and down at different rates – some slow, some fast. During ordinary waking consciousness, EEG patterns are complex, scattered and disorderly.

Typical EEG tracings

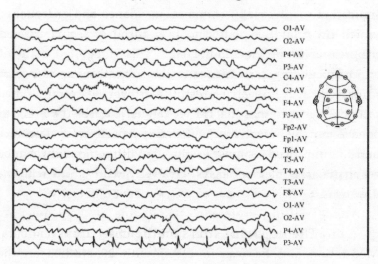

Increased EEG coherence
during Transcendental Meditation

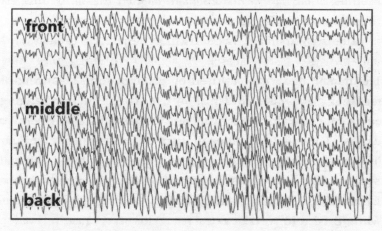

The second EEG chart is taken from a study published in *Cognitive Processing* in 2011 where 50 students were randomly assigned to one of two groups, either practising Transcendental Meditation or resting with the eyes closed.[15] The brainwaves rise up and down together – maintaining a stable phase relationship

– indicating that the whole brain is highly correlated. The significantly increased coherence in the alpha 1 frequency in the TM group, compared to the control group, confirmed the results of previous research.[16] This integrated state of brain functioning corresponds to the subjective experience of heightened wakefulness or restful alertness.[17] Several studies provide evidence that the TM technique cultures the brain to behave more coherently and efficiently over time, as seen in a person's improved response to stimuli – with better performance on spatial and memory tasks, creativity scores, and reaction time tests.[18]

The impact of stress on the individual

The European College of Neuropsychopharmacology has said that nearly 40% of the European population suffers from mental illnesses and that 'mental disorders' have become Europe's largest health challenge in the 21st century.
Lorenzo Marsili and Niccolo Milanese, *Citizens of Nowhere*

The human body is comprised of numerous self-balancing or feedback mechanisms which allow us to cope with the changing environment so that we can function in an optimal way wherever we are. These natural homeostatic mechanisms mean that our bodies exhibit a dynamic orderliness. When these internal regulating systems fail for any reason, we become unwell. When we are ill, in addition to any medication a doctor may prescribe, we will be told to take extra rest. This is because relaxation allows the body's homeostatic or self-balancing mechanisms to repair the body. Transcendental Meditation provides deep rest to the body while the mind remains alert, and this facilitates the healing process.

There is a double sense of the word stress in *Healing Social Divisions*. Firstly, it is external pressure, for example a sudden loud noise, and secondly, it is the impact on the human nervous system. Excess stress can lead to imbalances in our bodies; but we must distinguish between stress and stimulation. Stimulation or challenge will speed up brain processing. By stress I mean undue pressure of experience which leads to chronic activation of the stress response. If the challenge becomes too great then our fight-or-flight response kicks in. This is fine if you are in a dangerous situation, but problems come when the fight-or-flight response is triggered in more everyday settings and we react inappropriately. We can develop good or bad habits, and these habits strengthen neural circuits in the brain so that we respond to situations in an automatic way. This can be useful for a tennis player reacting to a powerful shot, but not if that aggression is channelled towards family and friends. If there is an over-activation of the stress response, it leads to an increase in cortisol and adrenaline. During Transcendental Meditation there is an increase in the orderliness of brain functioning whereas excess stress, not only in the case of PTSD but also with students, will reduce coherence in brain integration.[19] Everything we do, and what happens to us, impacts our brain, even if it is only minuscule, and that in turn will have an influence on our behaviour. Regular transcending is a way of resetting the brain to cope with the pressures of life.

More than 20 million dollars of research grants have been raised from the National Institutes of Health in the USA which have examined the effectiveness of Transcendental Meditation in reducing the risk factors associated with cardiovascular disease (CVD). The USA Department of Defense funded a $2.4 million dollar study, which was published in *Lancet Psychiatry*, showing the effectiveness of TM in reducing symptoms of PTSD.[20] There is currently research in nine hospitals in the USA on the effectiveness of Transcendental Meditation in reducing PTSD in war veterans.

Social benefits

I was initially sceptical, but having studied the research completed to date, I have concluded that these studies on the [Maharishi Effect] have subjected theory to proper empirical tests. They have shown sound results that demand serious interest. This method should be applied more widely in programmes to reduce crime.
Ken Pease, Visiting Professor at the Jill Dando Institute of Crime Science at University College London and formerly a member of the UK's Home Office National Crime Prevention Board, 1993–6

It is generally accepted that meditation can benefit individuals, but can it benefit society as a whole? There is a body of peer-reviewed evidence that indicates it can. Attempting to demonstrate cause and effect in society is fraught with difficulty. At any moment there are multiple sources of change and it is challenging to disentangle them and show a causal influence. Maharishi has given researchers the following hypothesis: "All occurrences of violence, negativity, conflict, crises, or problems in any society are just the expression of growth of stress in collective consciousness. When the level of stress becomes sufficiently great it bursts out as large-scale violence, war, and civil uprising necessitating military action."[21] The solution being proposed is this: as individuals reduce stress in their own brain physiology, this creates more coherence or harmony in the collective consciousness and influences the behaviour of those who are not practising Transcendental Meditation. This can be tested by measuring crime trends, acts of violence and various types of fatalities. In Chapter 3 we will explore whether this is anything more than a statistical correlation.

In 2020 we all became familiar with the idea of herd immunity. Many people who had the COVID-19 virus did not have symptoms but were still able to pass the virus to others.

Most of us do not commit crimes. However, we may still be suffering from an overload of stress – not so great that it leads us to commit crime but enough that we feel stressed and sometimes "get mad" with those around us and so create a tenser environment. The phrase "get mad" indicates that we are not acting in an appropriate way. The research on the Maharishi Effect provides evidence that it is the build-up of tensions and stress which is at the basis of crime and negative trends in society. When we reduce the tensions, we reduce the problems. Increasing the numbers practising Transcendental Meditation and its advanced programmes until we arrive at the appropriate threshold or critical mass is analogous to developing herd immunity in relation to negative social trends.

Why does transcending increase orderliness in brain functioning? Is it simply due to deep rest or is there a more fundamental explanation? We will come back to this question in the second half of *Healing Social Divisions,* but first I want to give a more detailed explanation of Maharishi's understanding of consciousness.

Chapter 2

Beyond language and ideology

For many literary professionals, words like unity, transcendence, spirituality, and consciousness have become an embarrassment.
Susan Seltzer and Terry Fairchild, *Consciousness and Literary Studies*

In his book *The Postmodern Condition: A Treatise on Knowledge*, the French philosopher and sociologist Jean-François Lyotard (1924–98) expressed scepticism towards what he called *grand narratives*. Grand narratives means big stories which purport to explain everything; examples could be religion, the Enlightenment, democracy or Marxism. In place of authoritarian, universalizing narratives, Lyotard recommends micro-narratives, none of which claim universal truth but rather are more culturally specific. The idea is that it is not possible to have a neutral vantage point; one's point of view will always be conditioned by historical, cultural, social and subjective factors. However, contrary to what Lyotard suggests, it is maintained here that rejection of universalizing narratives does not imply the rejection of universal truth. Maeve Cooke, Professor of Philosophy at Dublin University, suggests that one way to seek universal truth is to search for good reasons for beliefs through open-ended engagement with others who live their lives differently.[1]

Good reasons usually mean reliable evidence. Maharishi studied physics at university and not only did he encourage scientific research on the effects of Transcendental Meditation but he said its practice would involve the same principles as are found in modern science. Maharishi followed the development of unified field theory in physics, which is the attempt to describe all the fundamental forces of nature, and how they interact, in one theory. The idea of a unified field at the basis of all creation is a similar concept to that found in Vedanta, which is the conclusion of the six systems of Indian Philosophy.[2] On the basis of Yoga (the fourth of the six systems) and Vedanta, Maharishi was able to predict the benefits of Transcendental Meditation before any research had taken place. Yoga and Vedanta report experiences indicating that consciousness is more fundamental than we ordinarily assume and has a universal dimension. These philosophies have a different concept of the self from the current norm in the social sciences. *Healing Social Divisions* maintains that both views have their value, and that these different perspectives can be harmonized into a coherent whole.

It may be useful to clarify the following:

1. Is it possible to have an experience unmediated by language?
2. What is meant by the development of higher states of consciousness?
3. Testing Maslow's idea of self-actualization
4. The Buddhist conception of non-self
5. Is pure consciousness a universal experience; how does it influence behaviour?
6. Can the experience of pure consciousness be non-ideological?
7. What is the difference between collective intentionality and collective consciousness?
8. Is meditation merely an escape from the harsh reality of modern life?

Is it possible to have an experience unmediated by language?

Maharishi explains the practice of Transcendental Meditation as a process of "turning the attention inward towards subtler levels of

19

a thought until the mind transcends the subtlest state of a thought and arrives at the source of thought".[3] The source of thought can also be considered as the source of language, so when we transcend the process of meditation we are going beyond thought and language. (The deep rest gained during the practice results in clearer thinking and speech after meditation.) This may seem to contradict Lyotard, but it need not do so. Language-transcending experiences are possible and important. However, in many social contexts, we need or want to communicate these experiences to others using language, which is always conditioned by historical, cultural, social and subjective factors.

If one is not familiar with transcending space and time then it may be tempting to say that all experiences must be mediated by language and by events in life – that it is not possible to transcend language.[4] From the perspective of living daily life, it does not matter so much whether we say that experiences in meditation are or are not mediated by language as it is the benefits that are primary.

Transcendental consciousness has been described by people from different cultures at various times in history. Sometimes it is a result of a technique, sometimes it happens spontaneously, and in all cases it is independent of a person's belief or non-belief. Arthur Koestler (1905–83), the Hungarian journalist, former communist and atheist, who was imprisoned during the Spanish Civil War and eventually emigrated to the UK, had spontaneous experiences of transcending in prison which caused him some cognitive dissonance. He prided himself on his 'verbal precision' and he disliked 'nebulous gushings', and so he struggled to describe his experiences.

Koestler writes:

When I say "the I had ceased to exist," I refer to a concrete experience that is as verbally incommunicable as the feeling aroused by a piano concerto, yet just as real – only much

20

more real than any other one has experienced before – that for the first time the veil has fallen and one is in touch with "real reality," the hidden order of things.[5]

Koestler describes it as a process of "limitless expansion", and calls it "a river of peace, under bridges of silence". The expression *river of peace* captures both the idea of movement and stillness; there is silence and dynamism simultaneously. It is not a static state of peace but a lively state because it is consciousness being conscious of itself. On the one hand there is only consciousness, but on the other hand consciousness is in a self-referral state of being aware of itself; it is an eternal feedback loop of consciousness knowing itself. This state of consciousness on its own, because it is conscious, generates three values: a knower, a known and a process of knowing. The diagram below shows these three elements when we observe an object outside ourselves such as a flower. Consciousness, because it is conscious, can know itself; it is relational but it is relating to itself rather than something outside itself.

**The relationship of the knower,
process of knowing and the known**

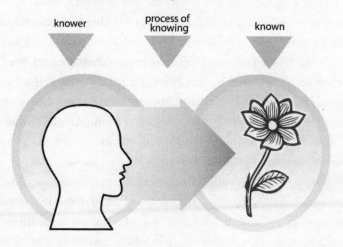

knower   process of knowing   known

Even before scientific research had begun on Transcendental Meditation, Maharishi commented:

> Any state of consciousness is an expression of a corresponding state of the nervous system. Transcendental consciousness corresponds to a certain specific state of the nervous system which transcends any specific activity and is therefore completely different from that state of the nervous system which corresponds to the waking state of consciousness.[6]

The scientific research provides evidence that a purely mental practice can change a person's physiology. The causal relationship between physiological functioning and consciousness flows in both directions: consciousness has its basis in physiology, and physiology has its basis in consciousness.[7] The implication of more than 400 peer-reviewed studies on Transcendental Meditation is that consciousness is more than an epiphenomenon of brain activity, a topic we will return to in Chapter 8.

According to the Swiss psychologist Jean Piaget, cognitive development culminates during adolescence in a set of abstract reasoning abilities, which Piaget describes as formal operations. This is the ability to work things out in your head without concrete aids. The psychologist Charles Alexander, who had been a post-doctoral fellow at Harvard University, co-edited a book with Ellen Langer, Professor of Psychology and the first woman to be tenured by the Harvard psychology department, called *Higher Stages of Human Development: Perspectives on Adult Growth beyond Formal Operations*. In the final chapter Alexander (et al.) discuss whether cognitive development is possible after adolescence. Alexander provides evidence that regular experience of transcending unfreezes adult development which has been blocked due to an overload of stress on the body. This results in human growth beyond formal operations. In the same way that language promotes development beyond the basic use of the senses, Alexander (et al.) are proposing that "exposure to a post language developmental technology – such as Transcendental Meditation...[facilitates] development beyond the language-based conceptual level of thought to post conceptual higher stages of consciousness".[8] The authors propose that just as humans have an inherent capacity for language which is actualized by "participation in a linguistic environment", so similarly, humans have a "capacity to transcend the thinking process" with the use of an appropriate technique.[9]

It is also possible to have such experiences spontaneously without any technique. The Jewish philosopher Martin Buber (1878–1965), who is known for his philosophy of dialogue, described his experience: "Now one is removed from the commotion, removed into the most silent, speechless heavenly kingdom – removed even from language."[10] Language helps us make distinctions; Koestler and Buber are trying to describe a reality where there are no distinctions, which is why it is said to be beyond language. The next section covers the development of higher states of consciousness.

Unfolding human potential

Maharishi describes the least excited state of consciousness as pure consciousness; pure because it is consciousness without any object of perception. He also describes it as Self-realization. The capital S is to make a distinction between Self and self. The Self is the experience of pure consciousness which is beyond language. The self with a lower case s is the different aspects of our self that are influenced by culture, language, social values, history and so on. This self is often described as relational and socially constructed. I will refer to the Buddhist conception of non-self in the next-but-one section.

Maharishi maintains that the Self, the experience of pure consciousness, is beyond all the relative changes in the world and is a state of non-change; as it has no content, there is nothing to change. Every person has a non-changing universal aspect and a changing particular aspect; we are simultaneously connected and separate from everyone around us. The self is bounded by all the various social and cultural influences whereas the Self is beyond those influences: we might say the Self is unbounded and the self is bound. An analogy may clarify this; a person at the top of a mountain will give a different description of reality from the person standing in the valley. It is not that one is false, but rather a different perspective. Maharishi uses the aphorism *knowledge is different in different states of consciousness* (see the Appendix). For example, the world appears differently to us after a good night's sleep and a bad night's sleep. This comparison is apt as the development of higher states of consciousness can be characterized as increasing alertness.

To clarify I will outline Maharishi's concept of the seven states of consciousness. This describes the expansion from the small self to the big Self. It is a process of growth, of unfolding human potential or unfreezing human development.

1. Deep sleep. A state of no awareness.

2. Dreaming. A succession of mental images, thoughts and emotions while asleep, where anything can happen. Physiologically, dreaming can be distinguished from deep sleep by rapid eye movements and different EEG patterns.

3. Waking state. This is our normal everyday activity when we are not asleep or dreaming. Within this there can be varying degrees of wakefulness or drowsiness depending on how well we have slept, what we have eaten, the pressure we are under, our general state of health and so on.

4. Transcendental consciousness. This is the least excited state of human awareness where we are awake but there is no object of awareness: we just are. It is consciousness on its own without an object of consciousness. Maharishi also calls this pure consciousness, the Self, Being, or pure awareness. The attention has turned from the outer world in an inward direction beyond sensory perception, thought, intellect and emotion. It is a state of pure subjectivity without any duality, meaning no object of experience.

Most of the research on Transcendental Meditation is related to the benefits people obtain after having experienced this fourth state of consciousness. It is quite common for new meditators to note an improvement in their relationships, with more tolerance and patience, and this happens spontaneously. They may express this as having more time or space and not being so reactive in their behaviour.

Pure consciousness is physiologically distinct from sleeping, dreaming and waking. It may be you are not convinced that the experience of pure consciousness is universal, beyond thought and not socially constructed; but whatever it is, it is something measurably different from sleeping, dreaming and waking. Those who do not agree with this description of pure consciousness need to supply an alternative way to explain the experience of pure consciousness and the scientific research on its effects on the individual and society.

The Scottish philosopher David Hume (1711–76) denies that it is possible to have an experience of an underlying transcendent Self or self. Hume writes:

For my part when I enter most intimately into what I call myself, I always stumble on some particular perception or other, of heat or cold, light or shade, love or hatred, pain or pleasure. I never can catch myself at any time without a perception, and never can observe anything but the perception.[11]

Transcendental Meditation takes advantage of the empirical methodology that Hume recommends and finds that the Self is not just "a bundle or collection of different perceptions", but if one has not had that experience then Hume's conclusion will seem valid. Without the experience, claims about pure consciousness may appear unintelligible.

Similarly, in their influential 1966 book, *The Social Construction of Reality: A Treatise in the Sociology of Knowledge*, Berger and Luckman claim it is only possible to experience consciousness of something and not consciousness on its own. This was the general view at the time, even though there was literature describing people having experiences of consciousness without an object. The former president of Egypt, Anwar Sadat (1918–81), describes his experience when he was in prison during the Second World War:

> Once released from the narrow confines of the 'self' with its mundane suffering and petty emotions, a man will have stepped into a new, undiscovered world which is vaster and richer. His soul would enjoy absolute freedom, uniting with existence in its entirety, transcending time and space. Through this process of liberation, the human will develops into love-force, and all earthly forces (even those that might perturb a man's mind) come to contribute to the achievement of perfect inner peace, and so provide a man with absolute happiness.[12]

Sadat, Buber and Koestler are examples of people spontaneously having transcendental experiences without any technique. Maharishi clarifies the role of meditation:

> Through meditation a situation is created where the Self is found uncovered, unfolded in Its pure and essential nature with no shadow cast upon It by anything. Meditation does

not unfold the self – the Self, it must be repeated, unfolds Itself by Itself to Itself. The wind does nothing to the sun; it only clears away the clouds and the sun is found shining by its own light.[13]

This process is sometimes described as a *pathless path* as the goal is already present at the beginning, as suggested in the description by Sadat.

Many people, whether or not they meditate, have a brief experience of transcendental consciousness at the onset of sleep which could be described as a junction point between waking and sleeping. EEG evidence supports the claim that these are physiologically the same experience.[14] This can be considered as a glimpse of transcendental consciousness which according to Maharishi underlies sleeping, dreaming and waking. Dr Fred Travis, an expert in EEG research during meditation, has described this as a junction point model of consciousness.

Travis was surprised to discover that the EEG patterns during Transcendental Meditation of those who had been meditating for eight months were no different from the EEG patterns of those who had been meditating for eight years. Travis had thought to himself, "They must get better at it." These results caused him a certain amount of puzzlement and he spent three months looking for the mistake he supposed he had made as this finding contradicted his expectations. Eventually he realized he had to accept the results and he understood how they needed to be interpreted. If one remembers that Transcendental Meditation is an effortless technique then, Travis realized, there is nothing to get better at.

5. Cosmic consciousness. At first the experience of inner silence is only experienced during meditation, as described in 4 above. With the alternation of regular meditation and normal activity this inner silence or Being begins to be infused into the mind.

When a person is never lost to that inner silence, Maharishi describes it as cosmic consciousness; by cosmic, Maharishi means inclusive of both the silent non-changing level of life and the active level of life. The transcendental state is eventually maintained with sleeping, waking and dreaming. One has realized the unbounded value of the Self which is maintained along with the changing bounded value of the self. It combines both the inner and the outer values of life; Maharishi has described it as living 100% of the inner value of life and 100% of the outer. From a philosophical perspective it is a dualistic state, Self and non-Self, and it represents the fulfilment of Yoga.

Travis looked at EEG printouts after practice of Transcendental Meditation and there was a difference between those who had been meditating for eight months and those practising for eight years. For the new meditators the distinctive coherence pattern in the alpha 1 frequency dissipated at the end of meditation; for the long-term meditators this unique EEG coherence pattern persisted. The difference was outside of the practice in terms of increased integration of brain functioning and is stronger the longer a person has been practising. Travis interprets these results as the growth towards higher states of consciousness. Alpha 1 brainwave patterns indicate alertness; Transcendental Meditation develops alertness and orderliness simultaneously.

We are all born in unique circumstances with our own individual backgrounds and genetic make-up. Some people will naturally display more orderly brain functioning than others, whether through nature or nurture. Transcendental Meditation stimulates human growth but it all depends from where one starts, so there is no claim that people who meditate are better than people who do not meditate.

Here is a description of cosmic consciousness from someone who learned Transcendental Meditation:

At first pure consciousness is experienced more as a backdrop to these changing states, a kind of screen against which all other things are experienced. But as it grows stronger, this abiding experience of pure awareness ultimately *eclipses* waking, dreaming and sleeping, which comprise what we thought of as living. They become so diminished as to be hardly recognizable as states of consciousness at all...And what's left is so much richer and more textured and fuller and more comprehensive and wiser and more stable and more filled with beauty than what you had before that it's like you are living life for the first time – like someone has turned on the light that *is* life and it can *never* again be extinguished. One now owns the very essence of life...

When one "awakens" in the morning, there is not the slightest change. It is always simply the Now moment, whether asleep or in the waking state. It is just the predominant awareness of Now, Pure Now if you will.[15]

There is some preliminary EEG evidence for this experience during sleep. The researchers found that the typical delta EEG patterns found during sleep were coexisting with the alpha 1 EEG patterns characteristic of the experience of transcending.[16] It as if the opaque curtains of the three relative states of consciousness are no longer opaque; they are transparent. The window which was wooden before has somehow been transformed into a glass window.

Transcendental consciousness or Being is spontaneously lived along with waking, dreaming and sleeping; it is not remembered on the conscious level of the mind "while engaged in thinking, speaking or acting". Maharishi continued:

Being is a state of life which cannot be lived by simply thinking about it. Being is lived naturally without having to think about it. The reason why we fail to live this natural state of Being is that we are not sufficiently acquainted with the transcendental field of life. The only way to achieve this is to transfer the attention from the gross to the subtle states of thought so that the field of Being is reached consciously.[17]

6. Refined cosmic consciousness. The emphasis here is more on the unifying values of the heart and greater appreciation of the environment, which is what we call love. Before cosmic consciousness, the Self is hidden from view by all the activity of the world. At first we experience the Self in meditation and then gradually that inner silence stays with us in activity until eventually there is a clear distinction between Self and non-Self, between silence and activity. The growth of the heart draws the two together. Maharishi explains: "It is this unifying factor of love that starts to function with great zeal and enthusiasm from the level of Cosmic Consciousness when the two aspects of life have been thrown apart – Self and the non-Self."[18]

These neat stages are somewhat artificial, and in reality one can have glimpses of any of these higher states of consciousness before they are permanently established. The sixth state is described as perception of the finest relative; a state where everything seems more alive. The poet William Wordsworth (1770–1850) gives a feel for it in 'Intimations of Immortality':

> There was a time when meadow, grove, and stream,
> The earth, and every common sight,
> To me did seem
> Apparell'd in celestial light...

Maharishi also describes these finer levels as celestial, but it is difficult to put into words. Lucy Maud Montgomery (1874–1942), famous for her *Anne of Green Gables* books, wrote in her autobiography:

It has always seemed to me, ever since early childhood,

that, amid all the commonplaces of life, I was very near to a kingdom of ideal beauty. Between it and me hung only a thin veil. I could never draw it quite aside, but sometimes a wind fluttered it and I caught a glimpse of the enchanting realm beyond – only a glimpse – but those glimpses have always made life worthwhile.[19]

Like the fifth state, the sixth state is also dualistic, the difference being that one experiences finer values of the non-Self; if one has not had the experience, one can only speculate about what it may be like.

7. Unity consciousness. After some time we start to perceive the environment in terms of our Self. Harmony rather than difference dominates the awareness. In his poem 'Tintern Abbey', Wordsworth gives us a hint:

And I have felt
A presence that disturbs me with the joy
Of elevated thoughts; a sense sublime
Of something far more deeply interfused,
Whose dwelling is the light of setting suns,
And the round ocean and the living air,
And the blue sky, and in the mind of man:
A motion and a spirit, that impels
All thinking things, all objects of all thought,
And rolls through all things.

Unity consciousness represents the complete expansion of consciousness when a person "'perceives the same' oneness of life through all the diversity of experience".[20] We do not try to cultivate a mood of unity or being loving, but this happens spontaneously as stress, which was previously constricting the heart, is dissolved. Dr Vernon Katz, who worked with Maharishi on the translation and commentary of the first six chapters of the Bhagavad Gita and produced two volumes of *Conversations with Maharishi*, describes the process of gaining higher states of consciousness. Here he is summarizing respectively the fourth, fifth and seventh states: "First, 'Oh I have found myself'; then, 'Oh, I am separate from all this around me'; and finally, 'Oh, I am one with what I am perceiving.'"[21] From a philosophical perspective, Unity is a non-dual or monistic state; our senses still perceive boundaries but the boundaries no longer dominate; the opaque becomes transparent; this is Vedanta. It gives us an expanded sense of Self and identity.

Note that Self-realization is the opposite of selfishness; it enlarges rather than narrows one's moral circle. It is the development of these higher states of consciousness that is at the basis of healing social divisions because they reduce fear; we do not feel threatened by the 'other'. When we are more at ease with ourselves, we are more at ease with others. We still appreciate and enjoy the rich variety of life, but harmony starts to dominate. The 'other' starts to become as dear to us as our own self, and social divisions are spontaneously and naturally reconciled; societies thus become more at ease with themselves. Cultural diversity is no longer a ground for suspicion of those who are different from us. Unity consciousness makes sense of and provides substance to the maxim *love thy neighbour as thyself*. In the Appendix I quote Federico Faggin, the inventor of the microprocessor, who had a brief and spontaneous experience which illustrates this.

Comparing methods of self-actualization

One hundred and thirty-five self-development outcomes resulting from the practice of Transcendental Meditation have been evaluated. I want to review one peer-reviewed study called *Transcendental Meditation, Self-Actualization, and Psychological Health: A Conceptual Overview and Statistical Meta-Analysis*.[22] We need to unpack the meaning of the title.

Abraham Maslow (1908–72), an American psychologist, introduced the term self-actualization as the highest level in a hierarchy of needs. Maslow described a hierarchy of needs as starting with satisfying bodily requirements such as food, clothes and housing, then safety, belonging, esteem and finally self-actualization. Self-actualization is about developing one's full potential, including "increased acceptance of self, of others, of nature; increased spontaneity; superior perception of reality; greatly increased creativeness".[23]

Maslow's hierarchy of needs

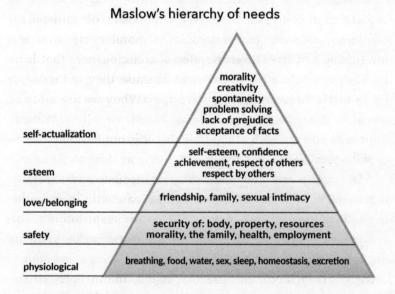

Maslow noted that self-actualized individuals tended to have peak experiences in which there is a loss of self or transcendence of it. Maslow conjectured that such peak experiences would benefit psychological health, increasing confidence, empathy and maturity. As a person increases in self-actualization, love becomes more dominant than fear.

A meta-analysis compares several already completed similar research papers in one study. For example, there have been several meta-analyses on Transcendental Meditation. Two measured decreases in anxiety, and another a reduction in substance abuse; all three found stronger results with TM compared to other methods of meditation and relaxation. In the meta-analysis on self-actualization there were 18 studies of TM, 18 of other types of meditation (6 Zen, 3 Relaxation Response and 9 miscellaneous treatments, such as mindfulness treatment, Yoga or mantra meditation), and 6 of other methods of relaxation (3 progressive relaxation and 3 miscellaneous).

The studies were compared in terms of their effect size. Effect size is a quantitative measure of the magnitude of the experimental effect; the larger the effect size, the stronger the relationship between two variables. On average, Transcendental Meditation had three times the effect size of the other procedures in enhancing self-actualization and its underlying components (emotional maturity, integrative perspective on self and world, and resilient sense of self). TM also led to significant improvements on each of the 12 scales of the most common test of self-actualization.[24]

The results of the meta-analysis suggest that regular transcendence increases self-actualization more than other methods of meditation which do not involve transcending. This analysis is supported by other studies that provide evidence for longer-term development of self-actualization as a result of Transcendental Meditation practice, by studies on prison inmates and on PTSD.[25] A meta-analysis from 2014, which only looked at randomized studies, showed a decrease in anxiety due to Transcendental Meditation compared with the control groups.[26]

Self-realization, the experience of pure consciousness, is the basis for self-actualization, but peak experiences may happen spontaneously and have been described by people from a wide variety of countries and historical cultures, independently of whether or not they practise any method of spiritual development. One example of this is the former basketball player and captain of the US team, Patsy Neal:

> I felt as though I was floating through the day, not just living it. That evening, when I shot my free-throws in the finals, I was probably the calmest I have ever been in my life. I didn't even hear or see the crowd. It was only me, the ball, and the basket. The number of baskets I made really had no sense of importance to me at the time. The only thing that really mattered was what I *felt*. But even so, I would have found it hard to miss even if I had wanted to. My motions were beyond my conscious control...
>
> I now know what people mean when they speak of a 'state of grace'. I was in a state of grace, and if it were in my power to maintain what I was experiencing at that point in time, I would have given up everything in my possession in preference to that sensation.[27]

Athletes often describe this as being in the zone; Maharishi describes it as spontaneous right action, a frictionless flow of communication and activity.

Fullness and emptiness

What the Vedantists call the Self (Atman), the Buddhists call non-self, and the Hasidim call the ayin are three perspectives of the same phenomenon: the egoless, timeless emptiness, the nothingness one finds when one looks for oneself.
Jay Michaelson, *Everything is God*

Maharishi contrasts the opposites of Self and self, unbounded and bounded. Buddhists talk about 'non-self', which is reminiscent of the views of David Hume that there is no unchanging, permanent self – which appears to conflict with the description from Maharishi. The different schools of Buddhism differ among themselves about how this should be understood. One interpretation could be in terms of simply letting go of the small self, as letting go is the way to experience transcendence. How should we describe that state of transcendence or what Buddhists call Nirvana? The following is an extract from the Mahaparinirvana Sutra, a Mahayana Buddhist scripture. Mahayana means great vehicle, a raft to cross the river of suffering.

> The monks were taken aback. They said, "Honoured One, according to all you have taught and spoken, we have been asked to cultivate selflessness, leading to the dropping of the idea of a self. But now you tell us we should cultivate the idea of a self – what is the meaning of this?"
>
> "Good," replied the Buddha. "You are now asking about meaning. You should know, that like a doctor, you should find the right medicine for an illness. It is as a doctor that I observed the ailments of the world. I saw that ordinary people believe they have a self and that whoever they meet has a self. They think of the self as within the body. But it is not like that. Because it is not like that, I have shown the fallacy of all the ideas of self and shown that the self is not there in the way it is thought to be...
>
> "But that does not mean that there is no self. What is the self? If something is true, is real, is constant, is a foundation of a nature that is unchanging, this can be called the self. For the sake of sentient beings, in all the truths I have taught there is such a self. This, monks, is for you to cultivate."[28]

This is identical to Maharishi's description: "It [the Self] is transcendental, ever the same, imperishable."[29] Both Maharishi and the Mahaparinirvana Sutra are relating the inadequacy of our everyday concept of self; after these limitations have been realized, how does one then describe the situation? Self and non-self are verbal labels and they could be different names for essentially the same experience but seen from a different perspective. Apparent differences of interpretation may simply be due to the difficulties of trying to use language to describe an experience that is abstract and beyond speech.

As these experiences are beyond language, some writings in Buddhist scriptures may appear at first as if they fall into Koestler's categories of verbal imprecision and 'nebulous gushings'. So, for example, this is from the Heart Sutra: "form does not differ from emptiness, emptiness does not differ from form. That which is form is emptiness, that which is emptiness form."[30] It sounds paradoxical, as when mystics talk about the emptiness of fullness and the fullness of emptiness. However, an analogy with the vacuum state in physics may clarify this.

Richard Feynman (1918–88), Shin'ichirō Tomonaga (1906–79) and Julian Schwinger (1918–94) jointly received the Nobel Prize in 1965 for their work in this field. The vacuum state in physics contains no real matter, light or excitation and is a quantum state with the least possible energy – it has zero entropy. One might describe it as a state of complete emptiness. Yet the vacuum state is apparently full of virtual particles; as they do not have a permanent existence, they are called virtual particles or vacuum fluctuations of vacuum energy. These virtual particles have been found to have measurable effects on actual particles to a high degree of precision.[31] The vacuum state is simultaneously empty and full. If we make an analogy, we can conceive of the Self as both full and empty; subjectively it is experienced as full even though it is devoid of content.

Maharishi also describes how the experience of Being or pure consciousness has been misunderstood in some traditional teachings of Yoga. The Yoga philosophy of Patanjali has often been interpreted as the eight steps of Yoga, but the Sanskrit word *anga* means limb, not step. When translated as *step* the experience of pure consciousness is understood to be the final stage of a sequence of steps, whereas limbs all grow at the same time. One starts with the experience of pure consciousness, and that drives the growth of all the virtues described by Patanjali, such as truth and non-violence and so on.

Maharishi was well aware that his teachings could, with time, also be misinterpreted and become a dogma. What would keep them fresh is the effortless experience of pure consciousness, but experience on its own is insufficient: it has to be balanced by understanding, which can come from several sources: empirical research, scientific principles and the traditional wisdom of humankind correctly interpreted.

Non-authoritarian authority

It is clear that ethics cannot be put into words. Ethics is transcendental.
Ludwig Wittgenstein, *Tractatus Logico-Philosophicus*

Although the experience of pure consciousness is universal, this does not make it an authoritarian ideology. The experience of pure consciousness is an individual's own most settled state of consciousness; it is not a form of external authority that is imposed on us and internalized by us. Part of the appeal of Transcendental Meditation is that it does not prescribe any code of conduct. People want to be free to make their own choices and find their own path in life. Authority can be authoritarian, be it the authority of the state, religious bodies, educational institutions or parents of families. It is authoritarian when it prevents individuals from working out for themselves what path they should take in life. It is non-authoritarian when it enables individuals to do this.[32] The practice of Transcendental Meditation could be described as a form of non-authoritarian authority.

Some feel the lack of traditional authority has given rise to a decline in standards. There is concern about growing narcissism and people focused on their careers and relationships and lack of interest in the world around them.[33] We cannot have an 'anything goes' attitude. Rather there has to be a recognition that some things are intrinsically of more value than others and this cannot be based on the fact that I value it. The Canadian philosopher Charles Taylor writes: "Self-choice as an ideal makes sense only because some *issues* are more significant than others...the ideal of self-choice supposes that there are *other* issues of significance besides self-choice."[34] By this he means that we choose in light of what he calls 'higher goods'; things that seem to us to be more important from the point of view of what is right and good.

Research on Transcendental Meditation among prison inmates gives an insight into this question of authority. There have been 20 studies that have found that the behaviour of inmates improves if they learn Transcendental Meditation. In some of these the TM group was compared with controls taking part in educational programmes, counselling, religious groups, and political and community groups. The research found that regular meditators benefited more than irregular meditators.

Three studies have measured a reduction in the reconviction rate for new offences after prison inmates had learned Transcendental Meditation. One of these consisted of 286 inmates released from Walpole maximum security prison in the USA, who were followed for up to 59 months.[35] The rate of return to prison for a stay of 30 days or more was 32% among inmates who practised the TM technique compared to 48% for a combined control group comprised of the programmes referred to in the previous paragraph. This is a reduction in recidivism of 33%; compared to all non-meditating subjects the reconviction rate for the TM group was 47% lower; these findings were statistically significant.

As this study did not have a randomized design, the extent

to which the findings can be generalized to other populations is limited. But the researchers did control for other variables that influence the likelihood of committing more crime: race, age at first arrest, employment history, drug abuse, prior adult commitment, release date, offence type, percentage paroled and age at release. This makes it unlikely that these variables can explain why there was a lower reconviction rate among the TM group compared with the control groups. Two other studies, which also found that Transcendental Meditation reduced rates of reconviction of former prisoners, statistically controlled for 28 background variables, including key predictors of reconviction rate.[36]

Those who learned Transcendental Meditation would have varied in their regularity of practice in prison, and once outside the prison gates we have even less idea of their constancy of practice; thus these studies would tend to underestimate the effect of Transcendental Meditation. It would have been explained that Transcendental Meditation provides deep rest to the nervous system, but such an intellectual explanation on its own is unlikely to have led to a greater reduction in reconviction rate than the four combined control groups. The former inmates had experiences of unboundedness, which then provided boundaries to their behavioural choices that had previously been lacking and helped to prevent them returning to prison.

Conduct became more law-abiding and changed as a result of physiological refinement without using any persuasion or codes of behaviour; Maharishi describes this as spontaneous right action. So without sacrificing their autonomy or freedom, these former inmates spontaneously began to behave in accord with the laws of the nation. The idea that the prisoners became more successful criminals and so avoided arrest is unlikely, as other studies had already shown improved behaviour in individuals while they were still prison inmates. In effect these prisoners gained moral insight, but not primarily through moral arguments either from others or themselves (these may have played a secondary role, perhaps unconsciously); rather, their moral insight came from having the experience of transcendental consciousness which influenced their biochemistry, for example by reducing cortisol which is related to high levels of stress. This was a process of physiological purification and internal authority; it could also be described as a reduction in physiological noise or disorder which leads to better decision making.

Approximately one third of the prison inmates who learned Transcendental Meditation went back to prison after committing a new offence. Learning Transcendental Meditation does not guarantee that a person will not commit crime; it only shows that they are less likely to go back to prison than other prison inmates in other rehabilitation programmes. Similarly with the research on self-actualization, it is showing trends and tendencies. Those who learn Transcendental Meditation come from different backgrounds, with different lifestyles and different genetic make-up, so there will naturally be variations in what happens after they learn TM. There is also the issue of whether someone who has learned TM is practising regularly or practising at all.

In 1987 Transcendental Meditation was implemented in three prisons in Senegal. The Director of Prisons, Colonel Mamadou Diop, noted dramatic results among the inmates within a few weeks: improved sleep, less aggressiveness, greater confidence, better relationships, improved health and reduced drug consumption; there was a decrease in fights, rule violations and escapes, and 70% fewer medical consultations. Here are some testimonials:[37]

TM must be the most effective method against drug abuse, because it helped me to stop smoking marijuana completely! The money I was spending every day for cigarettes or medicines (for my chronic bronchitis, my asthma, and rheumatism) can now be spent in a better way.

Inmate, Camp Pénal Prison, Dakar

My headaches are gone. Before TM, one of my shoulder blades would become painful at night. To my surprise, the pain disappeared from the moment I started TM.

Prison Officer, Thiès

My ulcer attacks have disappeared. I have had this disease for more than 10 years. I had used all kinds of medicine which had not brought about any improvement.

Prison Governor, Kaffrine

Since I started Transcendental Meditation, I no longer lose my temper so quickly. After each sitting, my mind is in a state of total peace; nothing disturbs it.

Inmate, Sébikotane

Meditation has made me harmonious, patient, wise, purposeful, hopeful, and reserved. It has facilitated the practice of my religion, and I'm very happy about that.

Inmate, Camp Pénal Prison, Dakar

Previously, every time I woke up, I was in a terrible mood. Now, it is the opposite. I wake up in the morning in very good spirits. The bad moods and quarrels are over, no rough times anymore. I live in perfect harmony with the inmates of the cell.

Inmate, Camp Pénal Prison, Dakar

Most psychological research is on people (often students) from WEIRD countries; western, educated, industrialized, rich and democratic. This was not true of this case study in a Senegalese prison. Due to the initial success, the programme was extended to an additional 28 prisons. In the second half of 1988, 2,390 prisoners were released in a presidential amnesty. Based on previous experience Diop would have expected about 90% to return to prison within two months, especially as there was a lack of employment opportunities; fewer than 200 went back to prison. Three prisons were closed for six months due to a lack of inmates, and eight others were operating at reduced capacity. The Greek philosopher Plato (424–327 BC) said that we can either be governed by a wise power within ourselves or alternatively submit to external authority.

Is everything ideological?

Maharishi's ideas come from the Vedic tradition of India, so how can I say they are not an ideology? Experience and understanding are both important and any form of comprehension will have a theoretical component. Can an experience be neutral or must it always be coloured by one's culture, language, values and historical situation? During Transcendental Meditation we experience finer values of a thought (only using the sound aspect of a thought without any meaning), until we go beyond the finest value of a thought and are left with consciousness or awareness on its own without any object of consciousness. When there is an object of consciousness, whether a thought or a sense perception, then that will be subject to a multitude of cultural and linguistic influences. In itself pure consciousness is inherently non-ideological, but the description after the experience could be dogmatic.

Maharishi describes the experience of pure consciousness or Being as abstract and not concrete, but:

The words abstract and concrete are relative, and neither truthfully expresses the nature of Being. But if, for the sake of understanding, we have to use a word to convey the nature

43

of Being, we can only say It is abstract and not concrete, even though the experience of It is far more concrete than anything in relative life. Because of its abstract nature, the study of Being has been shrouded in mysticism, and in consequence, for countless generations, the ordinary man has been deprived of the great advantages of living Being.[38]

A materialist might describe all this as nonsense; and it literally is *non* sense; it is beyond the senses, intellect and feelings. This experience beyond the senses and so on leads to human flourishing which can be measured; so perhaps not nonsense after all. An early study in the mid 1970s in Ontario, Canada, on high-school students, who were randomly assigned to one of three groups, provides preliminary evidence that it is the technique itself, rather than the theory or any code of behaviour, which is critical for the effects.[39]

Group 1: Learned Transcendental Meditation.

Group 2: Learned Transcendental Meditation plus the theory behind it known as the Science of Creative Intelligence (SCI). Note that SCI does not include a code of behaviour but rather principles of human development such as alternating rest and activity, every action has a reaction, and so on.

Group 3: Studied SCI only.

Group 4: A fourth group did neither course, and rather than random assignment, they were matched with the students in the other three groups by grades and sex.

Before the random assignment took place, the students from all four groups were measured on nine psychological measures: creativity, intellectual performance, complexity, conformity, energy level, innovation, self-esteem, tolerance and anxiety. Fourteen weeks later all the students were tested for a second time on the same measures. The results were that the students who had learned Transcendental Meditation either on its own or with the theory course showed greater improvement on the psychological variables than either of the two groups that did not learn Transcendental Meditation, with or without the theory.

Those who had just learned about the theory did not improve as much as either group 1 or 2 who had learned and practised Transcendental Meditation. There was no significant difference between the group that did the theory only and the group that did neither of the two courses of Transcendental Meditation and SCI. This supports the suggestion that the experience of transcending and its effects in daily life are not due to theory or philosophy. Hundreds of schools around the world have introduced Transcendental Meditation as part of their curriculum, particularly in Latin America, Nepal, India and Bali.

What is the difference between collective consciousness and collective intention?

Celebrity in football is the enemy of coherence – and in modern football coherence is what denotes the very best from the rest.
Jonathan Wilson, *Cristiano Ronaldo held Juventus back: just what do Manchester United see in him?*

The last 40 years have seen an academic interest in the concept of collective intentionality. By collective intentionality is meant the shared attitudes and actions of specific groups. Neither individual nor collective intentionality is a part of Transcendental Meditation. There is no intention to transcend, to have any particular kind of experience or any wish for social change during the practice itself. Outside of meditation a person's intentions will vary according to their background, upbringing and culture. There may be a collective intention for certain people to meditate together, but once they begin meditating they are not concerned with such intentions.

A collective intention theorist might say that a sports team is more than the sum of the individual players who make up the team; that the whole is more than the sum of the parts. Durkheim suggested that the collective consciousness is more than the sum of its parts and has a "life of its own".[40] That is, collective consciousness has a causal influence over and above the specific individuals who comprise a particular collective consciousness. We can think of a sports team as having a closer or more distant team spirit. This can be difficult to quantify, but every manager of a sports team knows it can make the difference between winning and losing. The stronger and more unified the bond between the individual players with their differing skills and specialities, the stronger and more successful the team. A sports team has a collective intention to win, but in addition to this intention, there is the degree to which they do or do not bond and harmonize together; that is collective consciousness. However, when we are talking about the Maharishi Effect there is a difference from a sports team. All the early research was on the effect of 1% of the population of a city learning Transcendental Meditation, and as a result, crime trends were beginning to decrease. Those people who learned Transcendental Meditation did not necessarily know each other and generally they would not have interacted with each other. The number of people who go to a meeting at their local TM Centre is a small proportion of those who learn; it is probably under 5%. They would have learned for a variety of reasons but mainly for personal benefit. It would be unusual for someone to learn Transcendental Meditation because they wanted to reduce crime, especially in the early to mid 1970s. As an individual becomes less tense, they contribute less stress into the environment, and that more settled, less excited atmosphere in the collective consciousness to some extent influences the behaviour of those who are not practising Transcendental Meditation. In these studies we are not talking about stopping crime, but rather decreasing or reversing trends. A more dramatic impact on crime would require larger numbers practising Transcendental Meditation as this would have a greater effect on the collective consciousness of a society.

Escaping the *iron cage of rationality*?

Max Weber (1864–1920) is famous, among other things, for the concept of the iron cage of rationality. This is the idea that modern scientific knowledge has replaced older forms of metaphysics, religion and spirituality, which have become regarded as superstitious, mystical or irrational. Society can become dominated by bureaucratic rules and this can result in fragmentation and a lack of meaning in life.

There may be a temptation to escape the iron cage of modernity by reintroducing some magic into the world, and Weber predicted that people may act wilfully and irrationally to re-enchant the world. They might turn to religion, or "seek transcendence in the aesthetic and sensual realms".[41] Some readers may want to categorize Transcendental Meditation generally, and specifically the Maharishi Effect, as an escape from the cruelty of the modern world, but consider the following four points.

1. Randomized scientific research on Transcendental Meditation provides evidence that it is not a placebo effect but changes can be measured compared with active control groups.
2. If the scientific research is showing real results from the practice of meditation then there must be a scientific explanation for these results, even if at present we do not yet have a complete account.

3. Maharishi did not use the term re-enchantment but he
    was very aware of the problem of wishful thinking, which
    he describes as mood-making. In his translation and
    commentary on the first six chapters of the Bhagavad Gita,
    which is known as the scripture of Yoga, he warns about
    mood-making 15 times. By mood-making, Maharishi means
    a person who is seeking to gain higher states of consciousness
    and pretending to be unaffected by pleasure or pain. This
    would:

    bring dullness, artificiality and tension to life in the name of
    spiritual growth; it has spoiled the brilliance of many a genius
    in every generation for centuries past. As a consequence,
    there has grown up in intelligent levels of society throughout
    the world a kind of fear of the spiritual life, which has gone
    so far that young and energetic people today find even
    discussion about spiritual practices embarrassing.[42]

Times have changed since Maharishi wrote this in the 1960s,
but even today it is still true that there are misunderstandings
and distortions about meditation; intellectual understanding
on its own is not sufficient, and direct experience of pure
consciousness is needed. Such mood-making may "result in
strange moods and stranger behaviour".[43]

4. Maharishi made it clear that spiritual development did not
    require detachment from life and emphasized that lack of
    spiritual development is not the fault of material progress
    and scientific achievements:

    If a man is inside a room lit by a candle with the doors closed,
    can we say that the candle is holding the man from opening
    the door and letting in the bright sunlight?...So it is wrong
    to blame the growth of modern materialism for the spiritual

degeneration of man.[44]

Transcendental Meditation harmonizes spiritual and material values by infusing pure consciousness or Being into the mind and then people will have the "experience of peace and spiritual joy in their daily life, and increase their energy".[45]

Thus the Transcendent is a state beyond language, without any ideology or intention, and its authority comes from moral insight rather than simply being imposed on a person: it can be described as the Self with an upper-case S. The process of transcending leads to more integrated brain functioning, which is at the root of all the benefits of Transcendental Meditation for the individual and society. In the next chapter we will examine evidence that Transcendental Meditation, practised by sufficient numbers, can reduce fatalities and violence, leading to more freedom, happiness and social harmony. Later in *Healing Social Divisions* I will explain how this experience of inner silence produces such a wide range of positive influences.

Chapter 3

Collective traumas and glories

Both read the same Bible, and pray to the same God; and each invokes His aid against the other.
Abraham Lincoln, Second Inaugural Address

The Lincoln quote refers to the American Civil War, and the words Bible and God could be replaced by the word constitution. The Confederates and the Unionists justified their actions as being in accord with the American constitution, those in favour of slavery pointing to property rights enshrined in the constitution and those against slavery referring to democratic rights of representation. Thomas Jefferson (1743–1826), who wrote the original draft of the American Declaration of Independence, was himself a slave owner; the USA may have been set up as a democracy, but no one voted to be a slave.[1]

After the civil war there were three major amendments to the constitution. The Thirteenth Amendment abolished slavery in the United States; the Fourteenth allowed everyone born in the United States (including former slaves) to be citizens with rights to due process and equal protection under the law. Finally, the Fifteenth Amendment, ratified in 1870, prevented the states from denying the vote to anyone based on race, colour or having previously been a slave. Despite these legal changes more than 150 years ago, racism is still a problem in the USA, which indicates that more than time and constitutional changes are needed to heal social divisions.

In August 2017, at a white supremacist rally in Charlottesville, Virginia, a 32-year-old woman was killed when a white supremacist from Ohio deliberately drove his car into a gathering of counter-protestors, an action for which he was subsequently found guilty and sentenced. Within three months of the killing, there were attacks on mosques, churches and synagogues in different parts of the world. At this time both the process of Brexit and the presidency of Donald Trump were causing deep social divisions. Professor Vamik Volkan, a psychiatrist and former medical director of the University of Virginia hospital, writes that whereas the founder of psychoanalysis, Sigmund Freud (1856–1939), looked at the influence of large groups on the individual, he himself explains about "large-group psychology *in its own right*", and specifically, collective identity.[2]

Since the 1980s Volkan has been bringing together participants involved in conflicts around the world. Volkan writes, on the basis of his "decades-long activities in the international arena", that more important than politics or economics "is the protection and maintenance of large-group identity…'We are Cypriot Turks,' 'We are Palestinians,' 'We are Lithuanian Jews,' 'We are Russians living in Estonia,' 'We are Croats,' 'We are Greek,' 'We are Communists,' 'We are Sunni Muslims.'"[3] Volkan uses a metaphor of different groups being together in their own unique group tents. Prejudices learned as children are then passed on through the generations. Rigid memories of past traumas, which may be hundreds of years old, can influence behaviour in the present, and when under stress people find security in group identities. These traumas may result in large-group regression, leading to fear and support for a strong leader with the attendant dangers of political and social manipulation. Volkan notes five steps in a leader's propaganda machine:

1. reactivating a chosen trauma;
2. enhancing a shared sense of victimization within the large group;
3. increasing a sense of 'we-ness' by returning to a chosen glory;

4. devaluing and dehumanizing the Other;
5. creating a sense of entitlement for revenge.[4]

When large-group progression takes place, attitudes change about the leader's propaganda, and more humane aspects of former enemies are appreciated. Volkan concludes with a plea for large-group psychology to be taken more seriously so it can contribute to making a more peaceful world. "People are busy asking a metaphorical question, 'Who are we now?' and coming up with seemingly opposite answers."[5] Even democracies may result in the tyranny of the majority and exacerbate the problem of social harmony.

From the individual to the group

Multilevel selection theory allows us to frame-shift the entire discussion upward, in which the wholes are social groups and the parts are their individual members...A position in the social sciences that in the past seemed wooly-minded and mystical can be placed on a rock solid evolutionary foundation.
David Sloan Wilson, *Darwin's Cathedral*

Research on Transcendental Meditation has measured improvements in 279 health outcomes in the following categories: health-care utilization (12), health-promoting behaviour (49), ageing (23), cardiovascular disease (66), general health (95), respiratory health (8) and rheumatology (26).[6]

Dr Norman Rosenthal, the psychiatrist who first diagnosed Seasonal Affective Disorder (SAD) and developed light therapy as a treatment, likes to quote research on the influence of Transcendental Meditation on 202 subjects who had previously participated in randomized studies on hypertension and were at least 55 years old at the time of the earlier research.

The team searched the National Death Index to determine which ones had died in the intervening years, along with their cause of death. The average time lapsed since the original study was 7.6 years, though some people had been studied almost 19 years before. Once the earlier studies ended, the researchers had no further contact with the participants, so there was no way to know whether those who had been taught TM had continued to meditate. Presumably some had not. Nevertheless, compared with the controls, *the TM group showed a 23% decrease in all causes of mortality and a 30% decrease in cardiovascular disease...*TM is as powerful as many of our best drugs without the side effects.[7]
(Italics in the original)

In 2013 the American Heart Association reviewed the evidence of the effects of various methods of meditation on reducing high blood pressure; based on the evidence, it referred to the effectiveness of Transcendental Meditation. It is the build-up of stress in individuals that flares up into problems, not only for the individual in terms of heart disease, but also for societies in terms of civil strife. This summarizes the problem outlined by Volkan in his recent book *Large-Group Psychology: Racism, Societal Divisions, Narcissistic Leaders and Who We Are Now*. Societal stress should be addressed from all possible angles. The process of Transcendental Meditation is one of letting go; in the case of individuals suffering from PTSD, there is often a problem of unwanted or intrusive thoughts as a result of a major trauma. The power of these thoughts, of these inner rigidities or boundaries, begins to lessen when a person practises Transcendental Meditation. As Volkan discovered, there can be rigidities and boundaries in the collective consciousness. The 50-plus demonstrations and the 150 measured outcomes of the Maharishi Effect provide evidence that these rigidities in both the individual and society can be reduced.

There are more than 25 demonstrations of decreasing crime and homicides, 12 demonstrations of reduced motor car accidents and fatalities, and 5 demonstrations of a decrease in suicides in society as a whole due to relatively small numbers practising Transcendental Meditation and its advanced programmes; and the greater the numbers, the bigger the effect. Independent research has shown that stress is connected with car accidents, and social cohesion is related to the incidence of suicides.[8] Studies on the Maharishi Effect have mainly been team efforts, and one included a non-meditating FBI statistician; more studies by non-meditating researchers would be welcomed.[9] In the first peer-reviewed study on the Maharishi Effect, an independent academic selected 24 control cities, which were compared with 24 experimental cities where 1% of the population were practising Transcendental Meditation. The research has taken place in different countries, on different continents, and at different times of the year.

Other studies on the Maharishi Effect have demonstrated decreased cigarette and alcohol consumption, not just in meditators, but among the general population. This and the other effects happen when the relevant threshold of either the 1% practising Transcendental Meditation or the square root of 1% practising the more advanced TM programme together in a group is surpassed. These tipping points of 1% and the square root of 1% should be taken as reasonably accurate guides rather than thresholds like the boiling and freezing points of water (and even these are not absolute). The Maharishi Effect does not replace conventional means of dealing with problems of crime, car accidents and suicide. However, one would expect government programmes and other proposed solutions to have more impact in tackling these issues when there is more coherence in collective consciousness.

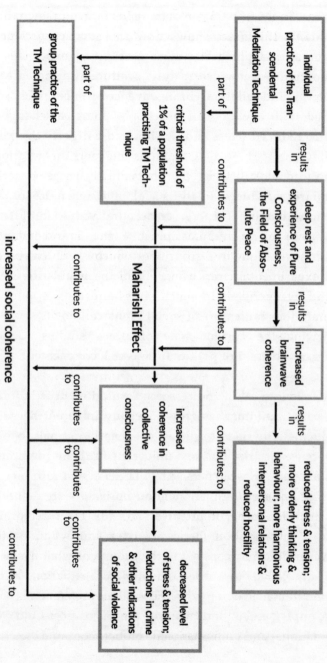

A schematic representation of the Maharishi Effect[10]

The top row in the illustration of the schematic representation of the Maharishi Effect shows how the practice produces deep mental and physical rest as a result of experiencing pure consciousness, which in turn produces an increase of homolateral and bilateral brainwave coherence (which is correlated with a variety of psychophysiological changes), leading to reduced stress and tension, more orderly thinking and behaviour, and more harmonious interpersonal relations and reduced hostility in the individual. These benefits are similarly produced in the social field when 1% of the population practise TM (i.e. create the Maharishi Effect, middle row) or individuals practise the Transcendental Meditation technique in a group (bottom row), which results in an increase of coherence in collective consciousness, as measured by decreases in social stress and tension, and in crime and other indicators of social violence.

Reviewing the current state of peace studies, Gerald Steinberg, a professor of politics from Israel, commented:

Academic interest in and research focused on peace studies and peace building has grown steadily in recent decades, producing a myriad of articles in scholarly journals, books, conferences, workshops, and university programs dedicated to this field. Researchers, practitioners, and officials of funding agencies – government and private – are naturally drawn to the hope or promise for finding a cure for the scourge of war, both between states and within states. However, in direct contrast to the growth of what has been cynically called 'the peace industry', the situation on the ground remains quite grim. Few stable agreements have been implemented, and many of the major post-Cold War international and ethno-national conflicts continue.[11]

David Edwards, Professor of Government at the University of

Texas at Austin, who has reviewed the studies on the Maharishi Effect, noted:

> The claim can plausibly be made that the potential impact of this research exceeds that of any other ongoing social or psychological research program. The research has survived a broader array of statistical tests than most research in the field of conflict resolution. I think this work, and the theory that informs it, deserve the most serious consideration by academics and policy makers alike.[12]

Do other types of meditation have this influence on conflict resolution? We don't know, as there has not been peer-reviewed research on whether other methods of meditation produce these large-scale sociological effects. In theory any method that facilitates transcending should have a positive influence on society.

Political violence

In a survey of 1,500 scientists in the journal Nature, *70 per cent of the respondents failed to replicate the findings of another scientist's experiment. Half of them couldn't even replicate their own findings.*
Richard Seymour, *The Twittering Machine*

Apart from death and grief, political violence creates fear and tension within society. The reduction of political violence and an increase in cooperation due to the Maharishi Effect has been demonstrated about a dozen times in some of the world's most intractable trouble-spots. Between 1982 and 1984 a prospective pilot study during the Lebanese civil war involved 1% of the population of the village of Baskinta learning Transcendental Meditation, leading to a dramatic decrease in violence and property damage compared with four neighbouring Christian and Muslim villages.[13] The amount of shelling in Baskinta completely ceased when the 1% threshold was reached, whereas it increased by as much as 40% in the control villages.

In August and September 1983 a prospective study took place in Jerusalem.[14] Due to work and family commitments, the number of meditators was randomly above and below the required threshold to create an influence on a composite quality-of-life index which included daily war deaths in the civil war in Lebanon. As the variations in the numbers were not under the control of the researchers, it cannot be described as a randomized study, but it was the next best thing. There was a statistically significant 76% decrease in war fatalities in Lebanon when the numbers in the Transcendental Meditation group were at their highest compared with when they were at their lowest during August and September 1983. The quality-of-life index and the size of the TM group were highly correlated.[15] The study and subsequent analyses controlled for other factors that may have been the cause of the improvement in the quality-of-life index: Jewish holidays, other holidays, temperature, weekends, military manoeuvres and political events (Menachem Begin (1913–92), the Prime Minister of Israel at the time, announced his resignation).[16] An organizer of the assembly mentioned to participants that when they had to leave to go back to work, the consequence was an increase in deaths in Lebanon. The late Professor Ted Gurr (1936–2017), Professor of Government and Politics at the University of Maryland, stated:

There is another, equally fundamental epistemological assumption in the sciences: if a body of evidence consistently and strongly challenges a theoretical position, we should be prepared to discard or modify the theory. After reading two versions of this manuscript, I think that is where we are at. It reports six discrete replications of the same social experiment – assemblies practicing TM – all of which coincided with positive effects, not merely statistically significant but substantively significant effects, on a variety of indicators of conflictual and peace-making behaviors in Lebanon. I can find no flaws of any kind in the methodology employed. The author(s) have designed the studies and analyzed the data in ways that answer all reservations I have had, and more. And the results are internally consistent (across assemblies, across indicators of the dependent variable, and across time) as well as being congruent with the theoretical argument.[17]

In response to critiques, lead researcher Dr David Orme-Johnson (et al.) produced two further papers confirming Professor Gurr's assessment that there were no "methodological flaws", plus he re-analysed the data, strengthening the original findings.[18]

The initial research was published in the *Journal of Conflict Resolution* and the editor, Bruce Russet of Yale University, commented:

the hypothesis seems logically derived from the initial premises, and its empirical testing seems competently executed. These are the standards to which manuscripts submitted for publication in this journal are normally subjected. The manuscript, either in its initial version or as revised, was read by four referees (two more than is typical with this journal): three psychologists and a political scientist.[19]

Russet quoted one of the peer reviewers: "If I apply the criteria I would normally use to judge any other example of 'traditional' research I would have to recommend publication."[20] We may dismiss one study as luck, two as a coincidence, but 50 deserves further independent investigation. Most of these studies cover relatively short time-periods; the exception is the time series analysis published in 2019, which found a 96% decrease in all violent acts between 1993 and 2008 in Cambodia compared with a baseline period, after Maharishi initiated an educational project involving the teaching of Transcendental Meditation and its advanced programmes.[21]

Ecuador is investigating the use of Transcendental Meditation for its armed forces, and Brazil and Colombia are using it in their military academies, as is India. In Ukraine the army has used Transcendental Meditation with those affected by PTSD. More than 100 US generals and colonels have learned Transcendental Meditation at the National Defense University in Washington DC. Maharishi's aim was for every country to create a prevention wing in the military: a group at least the size of the square root of 1% of the population was to be permanently established, practising the advanced Transcendental Meditation programme together in a group twice a day, to prevent the birth of an enemy.

Soldiers practising Transcendental Meditation

Increasing cooperation between antagonists in the Middle East

How far that little candle throws his beams! So shines a good deed in a weary world.
William Shakespeare, *The Merchant of Venice*
In April 1976 Maharishi was interviewed by Israeli journalist

Matti Golan, who wrote for the newspaper *Ha'aretz*. Many Israelis were learning Transcendental Meditation and it was the year before Anwar Sadat surprised the world and spoke to the Israeli Parliament. At the time, only one pilot project had been published about the effect of Transcendental Meditation on reducing crime; there was no research on its effects on political violence. About 23 minutes into the 50-minute interview, Golan asks how Transcendental Meditation could help Israel.[22]

Matti Golan (MG): I've listened to one of the tapes where you are describing how a nation should work towards a situation where it won't have to defend itself by making sure that the missiles will stay on the ground. In other words by making sure that the atmosphere will be different and there won't be any reasons for war. But in Israel in the Middle East we have a certain situation where the enemies are already there. It's not a matter of just now trying to create a new atmosphere. The atmosphere is already there and there were already four wars in the area and our neighbours are not willing so far to make peace with us. What would you then offer to Israel?

Maharishi Mahesh Yogi (MMY): Transcendental Meditation in Israel adopted by 1 or 2% of the population of the country and the attitude of the enemies around will change. This I am saying on the basis of what has been seen now in about 500 cities in the world today. When the number of people practising Transcendental Meditation rises to about 1% of a city population, crime rate goes down, the negative tendencies are neutralised, and sickness goes down and accidents go down.

MG: But in the Middle East we don't have any communications with our neighbours, none whatsoever, so how are we going to influence them?

MMY: See there is a word in physics: infinite correlation, infinite correlation. Now that quiet state of consciousness gained through Transcendental Meditation is infinite correlation, and in the infinite correlation level, that is from the level of pure consciousness, communication is most ideal, ideal in the sense that there is frictionless flow of message, frictionless flow of intention, of thought, that the thought makes its way without losing its energy on the way. No friction, frictionless flow and in this way whatever the people of Israel will feel, the nation, Israeli nation, whatever it will feel when 1% of the people, 2% of the people are practising Transcendental Meditation, whatever the intention, it will find its way in the hearts of all the people far and near. It's the whole consciousness, the quality of consciousness of the nation has to be built up, and what we will find is, enemies coming to shake hands bringing gifts and become friendly.

MG: This obviously cannot be achieved overnight, or over a month or over a year. What until then?

MMY: It can be achieved within a week. There is nothing today which can't be achieved and this we say on the basis of these, what I said about 500 cities in the world today have already shown statistics of crime, criminal tendencies going down. Enemy means this criminal tendency.[23] So if the criminal tendency of 500 cities can go down by 1% of the people practising Transcendental Meditation in other parts of the world why can't it happen in Israel.

MG: But the crime rate has gone down, if you apply it to war it will mean that we will not lose the next war 100% but lose it in 80% which is no good for us anyway.

MMY: No. If we find that some percent of the darkness can be removed by putting a candle, we put a few more around and we remove the darkness.

MG: How can this be? You say it can be achieved in a week. How can it be achieved in a week?

MMY: What is the population of [Israel]?

MG: 3 million.
(Author's note: the population of Israel and the surrounding occupied territories is now 13 million.)

MMY: What we need is 30,000.
(Author's note: 1% of the population is now 130,000 and the square root of 1% of the population is 400 in the case of a group practising the more advanced Transcendental Meditation programme; this practice was introduced a few years later. If one was to include the populations of Egypt, Lebanon, Jordan and Syria, the numbers needed would be larger.)

MG: And this will achieve, this will affect the Arab...

MMY: It will affect the tendencies, the thinking, the understanding, the emotions of not only those who are supposed to be the enemies of Israel today but even the friends of Israel. Israel must have understood, must have experienced, that friends today may not be a friend tomorrow when the need for friendship comes. All this friendship and enmity is a very volatile reality. Just as friends can be non-friends tomorrow, enemies can be non-enemies tomorrow. It is only a matter of the quality of national consciousness which can be raised overnight.

MG: To be on the safe side we would like to have a counterpart to govern the Arab countries though, we would like them to have the 1% as well. As far as I know there is...

MMY: Arabs or whatever, other countries. It is just the thinking and if in a community 1% of the people practising Transcendental Meditation can quietly change the attitudes of the criminals. Next day they come out. Maybe when they went to sleep they were thinking of making a plot against that person. In the morning they come out, they forget about the plot. If they meet him on the road, shake hands. He is a friend now. If this miracle can be created in a community, the same miracle can be witnessed in any country today.

MG: But this is in a community where they live together, where they communicate, it's the same city or the same country. In Israel we have no communication with our neighbours whatsoever. The borders are closed. No Arab is coming from the Arab countries to Israel and no Israeli is going to the Arab countries.

MMY: No, no.

MG: How is Israel going to influence over the border?

MMY: No. Borders don't exist today in reality. They are only a kind of psychological thing. The border could remain here. You can take a helicopter and go behind the border. The border doesn't...

MG: If you go behind the border in a helicopter in the Middle East you don't come back.

MMY: (Much laughter) Then we don't go till we are invited on some celebrations. 1%, give me 1% of the people meditating in Israel and I give you the whole of the Middle East.

How did Maharishi know Transcendental Meditation could have this effect on political relations in advance of rigorous research? Remember he had predicted this influence in 1962 before there was even any research on the benefit of TM for the individual. The concept of infinite correlation that Maharishi refers to in the dialogue with Golan may be found in physics, but this only confirmed what Maharishi knew from Vedanta that everything is connected, an idea found in many cultures. The implication is that consciousness is analogous to field effects found in physics, something spread out in space and time. Given this fundamental connectivity and harmony, if it is possible to enliven that through Transcendental Meditation, then this should in theory increase the harmony on the surface of life. It is analogous to dropping a stone in a pond and seeing the waves spread out. The peer-reviewed research on the Maharishi Effect provides evidence for both this connectivity and that transcending can increase orderliness or coherence in collective consciousness.

It is not uncommon in science for an increase in orderliness in a small proportion of a population to trigger an increase in order in a whole system. An example is when 1% of cardiac muscle cells, known as pacemaker cells, spontaneously generate electrical impulses. Similarly, relatively small numbers practising Transcendental Meditation seem to influence the whole of society; and the larger the numbers, the bigger the impact.

We often see dictatorial governments and rebel groups around the world treating minorities and sometimes children in war zones in cruel and wicked ways. Maharishi was predicting that a sufficient increase in the coherence of collective consciousness would influence their thinking and, just like the former prison inmate and the war veteran suffering from PTSD, political leaders would start to make different decisions. The 2020 pandemic has shown that borders are a human construct created in people's minds. With the virus, governments can ban travel; it is not possible to stop the effect of enlivening Transcendental Consciousness from spreading. It is the same harmonizing influence, whether we are considering divisions within or between nations.

"Seven times gets your attention"

John Davies is co-director of the Partners in Conflict and Partners in Peacebuilding Projects at the University of Maryland. Together with Charles Alexander, he repeated and extended the 1983 Jerusalem research. Based on daily data, they investigated the effect of seven Transcendental Meditation peace assemblies, held between the summer of 1983 and the summer of 1985, at different times of the year, lasting 93 days, compared with 728 control days when there were no such assemblies.[24] They were held in different locations around the world and with varying numbers of participants, but all large enough to have an influence on the conflict in Lebanon. They measured statistically significant decreases in war deaths, war injuries and intensity of the conflict, and in addition an increase in cooperation between the antagonists; the results were stronger when combined in a composite peace/war index of all four variables.

The violence was not just between Israel and Lebanon, but there were also deep splits between Sunni and Shia Muslims, Greek Orthodox and Maronite Christians, as well as involvement from Syria and the Druse population – entrenched divides going back many centuries. In five of the seven assemblies there was a statistically significant improvement in cooperation between antagonists. During the whole two-and-a-quarter-year period of the study, there were almost constant efforts among at least some representatives of the parties to create peace.[25] The peace-keeping and violent events were not measured by Davies or his co-researcher Alexander; they were recorded by an independent, expert coder of events, who was blind to the purpose of the study. Improvements towards reconciliation occurred when the assemblies were taking place and, once the groups went home, events fell back into the same low pattern of cooperation as before the assembly.[26] Problems such as climate change, pandemics, nuclear weapons, tax evasion, social media, and so on, require international cooperation; this study and the related research give an insight that increasing coherence in collective consciousness could help to resolve these issues.

The researchers used statistical methods of an interrupted time-series design to eliminate the possibility that the results were simply reflecting pre-existing trends; they controlled for temperature and religious holidays; the assemblies were held at different times of the year, ruling out seasonal explanations; and they were arranged a long time in advance, so the organizers would not have known about the political situation at the time of the assembly. To safeguard against bias, the researchers employed independent news sources and independently developed scales of measurement, and the hypotheses were announced prior to the assemblies.

Davies and Alexander concluded: "The stronger effects seen for the composite index (and also when all assemblies were combined) support the interpretation of an underlying influence of coherence being produced in, and adding constructively across, diverse systems simultaneously."[27] The Canadian sociologist Mark Novak commented: "The repeated effect is persuasive. You might discount it once or twice but seven times gets your attention."[28] Freedom and happiness are severely constrained during a civil war; anything that can contribute to creating peace should be investigated.

A recent book, *Friendly Fire: How Israel Became Its Own Worst*

Enemy by Ami Ayalon, a former commander of the Israeli navy and then head of the secret service for internal security, attributes the deeply rooted conflict between Israel and the Palestinians to the entrenched narratives that each side in the conflict carries in their heads. Similarly, Steve Killelea, founder of the Global Peace Index and the Institute of Economics and Peace, reports that since 2004 the West and the Russians have had opposing narratives about the conflict in Ukraine and says there is a "need to transcend these narratives if we are to find peaceful solutions that encompass all".[29] Ayalon and Killelea are alluding to a mental rather than a physical cause such as land. It is the way of thinking of the two opposing sides, which implies that the solutions have their roots in consciousness.

Correlation or causation?

No physical or biological laws govern human behaviour exactly. Humans by nature are moody, petulant, haphazard, and adaptive. Statisticians build models to get close to the truth but admit that no system can be perfect, not even causal models...[but] models based on correlations can be very successful.
Kaiser Fung, *Numbers Rule Your World*

How can we be sure it wasn't just a coincidence that violence decreased and cooperation increased when the relevant threshold of the number of meditators was surpassed? The fact that two things happen together does not mean that one is causing the other. Here are 11 reasons why creating coherence in collective consciousness and social improvements are likely to be more than a statistical correlation and are consistent with a causal explanation.

1. The most important reason is repetition of research, and governments could undertake their own research to confirm

previous investigations. There have been 20 peer-reviewed studies and 50 demonstrations of the practice of Transcendental Meditation and its advanced programmes which have measured decreases in fatalities, violence, crime and so on; more than 150 outcomes in total. Papers have been published in peer-reviewed journals such as *Journal of Conflict Resolution*; *Social Indicators Research*; *Journal of Mind and Behaviour*; *Journal of Crime and Justice*; *SAGE Open Journal*; *Psychology, Crime & Law*; *Journal of Offender Rehabilitation*; and the *Journal of Social Behaviour and Personality*. Many of the original papers can be found online at www.anantidotetoviolence.org under the Further Reading tab.

2. Data was collected independently of the researchers, often by governments or other institutions depending on what variable was being measured; assessor blinding is thus built into the research. In one study a researcher was a non-meditating FBI statistician, and others have involved independent review boards.

3. In the Israel study referred to above, a diligent peer reviewer asked the researchers to do some extra statistical tests to double-check that the increase in the numbers of the TM group led the social changes rather than the other way round. This would exclude the idea of reverse causation, which may suggest that an increase in violence led to an increase in the numbers meditating. The results indicated that the relationship between TM and violence was consistent with a causal interpretation: meditation was leading the decrease in crime. The peer reviewer concluded: "the introduction of transfer functions, serves to further emphasize the hypothesis that the number practicing TM influences conflict/coherence, and not the other way around."[30]

4. There is a dosage effect. The larger the number of practitioners of Transcendental Meditation, the greater the effect, which suggests a causal influence.

5. There are many factors that influence crime and violence. In many of the studies, other variables have been examined to check they were not the cause of the measured changes. These include population density, median years of education, per capita income, percentage of people in the age range 15–29, percentage unemployed, percentage below the poverty line, percentage of people over 65, the ratio of police per population, weather, holidays, seasons, and political events. None of these other factors could completely explain the results of the research. Raymond Russ, PhD, Professor of Psychology at the University of Maine and former editor of the *Journal of Mind and Behaviour*, commented:

The hypothesis definitely raised some eyebrows among our reviewers. But the statistical work is sound. The numbers are there. When you can statistically control for as many variables as these studies do, it makes the results much more convincing. This evidence indicates that we now have a new technology to generate peace in the world.[31]

6. In many of the studies, the measured changes were predicted in advance and of course Maharishi first predicted this influence in 1962. The demonstrations have taken place in 14 different countries, on different continents at different times of the year, thus ruling out geographical or seasonal explanations.

7. Sometimes the numbers practising Transcendental Meditation fluctuated randomly above and below the required threshold postulated to produce an effect during the period of the research. When the numbers were above the required threshold there was an influence on social trends, but not when the numbers were below. Although the randomization was not under experimenter control, this 'virtual randomization' strongly suggests a causal relationship.

8. The results are statistically significant, and the statistical

significance in some cases has been extraordinarily high.[32] Also the effect sizes are often large, which provides evidence for a strong relationship between the practice of Transcendental Meditation and its advanced programmes and the improvement in social trends. Ken Cavanaugh, an expert on the Maharishi Effect, notes: "Much more important measures of the practical significance of a particular finding, such as reductions in homicide rate, is the percentage reduction in the rate and the estimated number of homicides averted or, to give another example, a 76% reduction in war deaths, etc. These are much more salient and easily understood indicators of whether the effect is not just statistically significant but practically or substantively important."[33]

9. Researchers have used sophisticated methods of time series analysis and strictly mathematical criteria to choose the best model to avoid suggestions of statistical manipulation or bias.

10. Several respected and independent academics have commented on the quality of the research on the Maharishi Effect. The researchers themselves had studied at top US universities such as Harvard, Yale, Princeton, Massachusetts Institute of Technology, Stanford, Columbia and also non-US universities.

11. In several studies, normally unconnected variables all improved at the same time, which gives us confidence there is a common influence. Given the above points, it would be challenging to think of an omitted variable that was responsible for the fluctuations in the numbers practising Transcendental Meditation and the improvements in a wide range of social variables.

It is not being claimed that Transcendental Meditation was the only cause of the social changes, but points 1–11 give us confidence that these correlations are consistent with a causal interpretation.

Turning the tap on and off

You – like all organisms – are a complex adaptive system. So is the World Wide Web. So are brains, termite colonies, swarming bees, cities and financial markets – to name a few. Within complex adaptive systems, small changes can bring about large effects which can only be observed in the system as a whole.
Merlin Sheldrake, *Entangled Life*

At the end of 2006 the coherence-creating group of those practising the advanced Transcendental Meditation programme in Fairfield, Iowa, increased from a few hundred to about 2000 when Maharishi asked some experts in this technology of peace, who normally lived in India, to join the group. Four studies by Cavanaugh and Dillbeck examined decreases in homicide, crime, fatal car accidents, other accidental deaths, infant mortality and deaths from opioids in the USA.[34] These six variables are mostly unrelated, with their own drivers for rises and falls, yet they all moved in the same direction in the period 2007–2010 compared with the baseline period 2002–2006. The researchers controlled for other variables that could have been the cause of the changes: unemployment, incarceration rates, temperature, policing strategies, urban demographics, social media, police technology, police reporting, number of miles travelled, weather patterns, proportion of young drivers, improved vehicle safety features, alcohol consumption, national economic conditions, increased public and professional awareness of the risks of opioid addiction, and sales of painkillers.

The solid line in the chart below shows the fluctuations in the number of people in the group between 2000 and 2016. The chart is split into three sections; a baseline period of 2000–2006 when the numbers participating were low, an experimental period of 2007–2010 when they were high, and a post-experimental period of 2011–2016 when the number of participants decreased after the money to support the group from India ran out and they had to return home. The different types of fatalities and crime were formed into a composite index, which is the line with the short and long dashes. In the baseline period there were small up-and-down movements, followed by a dramatic decrease in fatalities and crime during the experimental period and an increase in the post-experimental period. The only exception was for deaths from opioids, shown by the line with the even-length dashes, which were rising sharply in the baseline period, then levelled off between 2007 and 2010, and then increased even more sharply in the post-experimental period when the Indian section of the group returned to India.[35]

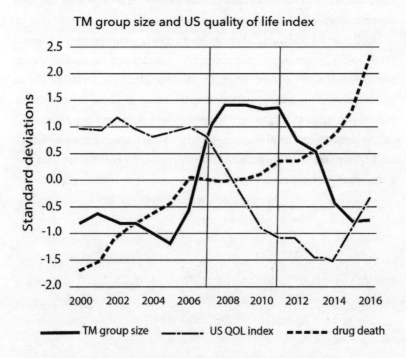

It is like a tap: increase the size of the Transcendental Meditation group and negative social trends decrease; turn the tap off by reducing the size of the group and deaths and disorder increase. Dr Orme-Johnson calculated the difference between what happened during the experimental period and what would have been the situation if the baseline trends had continued as in the pre-experimental period, in order to estimate the number of murders, car deaths and so on that were avoided. These were 11% fewer losses from infant mortality, 15% lower from drugs, 16% less from murder, and a 21% reduction in vehicle fatalities, which respectively translates into 280,516, 79,940, 28,333 and 95,885 fewer deaths than would otherwise have been expected. While we will never know for sure how many extra deaths would have occurred without the coherence-creating group, we are possibly talking about a few hundred thousand. This strengthens the case for causation rather than correlation, but more research would yield increased confidence.

Retired Lt Gen. Clarence McKnight, who was a former Director of Command, Control and Communications Systems for the Joint Chiefs of Staff in Washington DC, said: "I was initially skeptical that such a simple solution could be effective. However, after examining the evidence, I changed my mind...[it is] an unconventional but effective peaceful solution to violence and terrorism."[36] Being alive is a prerequisite for liberty and the pursuit of happiness.

Chapter 4

Varieties of freedom

Historically, pandemics have forced humans to break with the past and imagine their world anew. This one is no different. It is a portal, a gateway between one world and the next. We can choose to walk through it, dragging the carcasses of our prejudice and hatred, our avarice, our data banks and dead ideas, our dead rivers and smoky skies behind us. Or we can walk through lightly, with little luggage, ready to imagine another world.
Arundhati Roy, Indian writer

Maharishi does not advocate suppressing desires, as that "can only weaken all phases of life, material, mental and spiritual".[1] Experiencing pure consciousness is like removing the darkness in a room by adding light; with greater mental clarity we spontaneously tend to desire more life-supporting choices for ourselves and the world around us: "Man's life is so highly evolved that he enjoys freedom of action in nature. This enables him to live in any way he desires, either for good or for evil."[2]

In this chapter I will discuss the influence of Transcendental Meditation on internal constraints on freedom, freedom from external restrictions, creativity, and freedom from economic deprivation.

Internal constraints

We may be free in theory, but if we lack confidence or are suffering from intrusive thoughts as a result of PTSD, this will influence our behaviour. An extreme example is the serial killer Charles Whitman (1941–66). In his final letter before he went on his killing spree, Whitman asked for an autopsy to see if there was anything physically wrong with his brain that could account for his persistent violent thoughts and the painful headaches he was frequently experiencing. After the autopsy, they "found a tumour lodged inside his brain".[3] The difference between Whitman's behaviour and our own is a matter of degree. We may not have a tumour, but if there is some physiological deficiency, whether it is sleep deprivation, which has mental correlates, or severe depression, which has physiological correlates, this may result in us contributing increased tension to the collective consciousness of our society.

To some extent, these physiological restraints result in less freedom of choice for a person. To the degree that we are not suffering from these problems, we can say we have an increase in freedom. So any therapy or methodology that can help would increase a person's freedom, whether it is counselling, medically prescribed drugs or Transcendental Meditation. There have been 25 studies indicating a reduction in substance abuse, 20 studies demonstrating improvements in the behaviour of prison inmates, and 14 studies showing a reduction in symptoms of post-traumatic stress disorder due to Transcendental Meditation.[4] Maharishi comments:

If a man is wearing green glasses he can only see green. If a man has stresses and strains his consciousness can only be restricted. All these conflicts that come only from the narrowness of vision. A man can only see a small amount and so he focuses on himself too much. He gets blinded to all other areas of concern. This stubbornness, this rigidity, this arrogance is the cause of the eruptions of non-peace all over the world…All that is necessary is to raise the consciousness of the people, let them grow in the abilities of stability and adaptability, of purification and integration, and then the awareness of all the people will be able to reconcile between the local interest and the universal interest.[5]

With respect to freedom, is there any difference between Transcendental Meditation and other therapeutic modalities that enable a person to cope better with fear and stress? When we transcend the process of meditation, there is consciousness but no object of consciousness; we have transcended the finest value of a thought. While we are experiencing a thought or have any sensory perception, there is a boundary. Any boundary constrains freedom. When we transcend boundaries such as a thought, we experience a state of unboundedness or pure consciousness; it is a state of pure freedom. A person practising Transcendental Meditation may only have this experience to a certain degree, but this is enough for military veterans to find that symptoms of PTSD begin to improve within a relatively short time. The development of higher states of consciousness is known as liberation; liberation is not a fortunate by-product – it is the essence of the procedure. A person may learn Transcendental Meditation to be less anxious or to sleep better or to be more creative or more patient; this is accomplished by transcending, increasing their freedom from boundaries, which is an expansion of consciousness.

Rigid boundaries lead to constricted vision, to problems and suffering. These narrow boundaries may come not only from traumatic experiences but also from our upbringing and a restricted group identity. Recent research by Dr Leor Zmigrod at Cambridge University found that mental rigidity is associated with extreme beliefs and ideologies.[6]

Another quality that has been found to increase among those practising Transcendental Meditation is field independence.[7] Field independence means that a person is less dependent on external signals but takes their cue more from internal signals: they have a more stable internal frame of reference. Field independents tend to have a greater interest in being active and undertaking responsibility. Field independence is also correlated with creativity; it indicates the growth of freedom from boundaries. In Chapter 2 I referred to new meditators describing their experience outside of meditation as if they had more time and space; they are less reactive; this is equivalent to having more freedom. It would be interesting to investigate whether the development of field independence makes a person more resistant to external propaganda and manipulation.

Minimal external constraints

John Stuart Mill (1806–73), the philosopher and political economist, is famous for his essay *On Liberty*: "The only purpose for which power can rightfully be exercised over any member of a civilised community, against his will, is to prevent harm to others. His own good, either physical or moral, is not a sufficient warrant."[8] Effectively, Mill is asserting the absence of interference with another person unless it would lead to the harm of others. (One can of course query exactly what counts as *harm* in Mill's account.) The idea is that a person should be governed by external forces as little as possible. This is the essence of negative liberty in the political sense; an absence of constraints.

Mill gives four reasons why we should value the freedom of thought and speech of others who may hold different views from ourselves.

1. We are not infallible and we may be mistaken.
2. Other opinions may contain a grain of truth.
3. Even if we are correct, challenges to our point of view allow us to better understand the grounds for our beliefs.
4. Without challenges, there is a danger that our beliefs will become a dogma.

Mill, however, justified British colonialism, 'civilizing' the native inhabitants and modifying the established culture. While Mill's opinions were well intentioned, we now regard colonialism as a gross imposition of constraints by one nation on another. Today we accept that a person cannot be free if they are subject to unjustifiable discrimination, and I will have more to say on this in chapters 6, 7 and 9.

Freedom and happiness will be limited when a country is at war. In Syria half of the 22 million population have been displaced, including 6 million who have sought asylum overseas; this conflict has had repercussions not only in the Middle East but throughout Europe with the ongoing refugee crisis. Widespread practice of Transcendental Meditation can create the right conditions for political freedom and the pursuit of happiness. Governments will often use outbreaks of violence and war to justify restrictions on freedom; if there is less violence and war, the basis for this justification disappears. Restriction of freedom has its origin in fear; just as Transcendental Meditation dissolves stress in the individual, it will also reduce collective tensions, so providing the conditions for a free society. It is predicted that with permanent peace-creating groups, leaders will make decisions that benefit the whole population rather than particular sections.

Biochemical connectivity and freedom of choice

Individual stress can be measured in terms of biochemical changes; cortisol, a hormone associated with high levels of stress, decreases during the practice of Transcendental Meditation.[9] Similarly, there is some evidence that a decrease in collective stress has biochemical correlates in people who do not practise Transcendental Meditation. Preliminary prospective research has found that cortisol decreases and serotonin increases in people who live within the vicinity of a large Transcendental Meditation coherence-creating group but who do not practise themselves. The changes in the size of such a TM group have been correlated with changes in the levels of cortisol and serotonin and the ratio between the two biochemicals in non-meditators. The researchers used a wide range of diagnostic and statistical tests, and two other studies found similar results.[10] They checked that their results were not due to differences of behaviour at weekends. Higher stress might have been expected during the week than at weekends; if TM attendance was higher at weekends, this might give a false correlation. In fact TM attendance was lower at the weekend, and formal statistical tests confirmed that the weekend hypothesis could not explain the results. This helps us to begin to understand the mechanism of the Maharishi Effect in terms of how it neutralizes stress in collective consciousness, even among those who do not practise Transcendental Meditation.

Perhaps changes in the weather could explain the decrease in cortisol, the increase in the metabolite of serotonin, the increase in the size of the TM group, and the fact that the change in the size of the TM group was leading the biochemical changes. The weather hypothesis, however, was not supported by the empirical evidence. Ideally, a randomized study would provide stronger support for a causal connection.

The above research and other studies on the Maharishi Effect provide evidence that practising Transcendental Meditation can influence the physiology and behaviour of those who may otherwise have committed crimes. Let us put aside for one moment the ethics of committing crimes. One could say that the criminal's right to make their own choices is being interfered with by others, without their consent, and this could be seen as an intrusion of their freedom. This argument is mistaken for at least two reasons.

1. When a person practises Transcendental Meditation correctly, they have no intentions for anything; no intention to transcend, no intention to meditate correctly, and no intention to influence anyone; they are just innocent about the whole process, which is the key to its effectiveness.

2 Whether a person does or does not meditate, we all influence the collective consciousness of the society in which we live. Our every thought, word and action has some influence on our surroundings, whether we give someone a black look or a smile. Some actions create more tension in the collective consciousness and some less. And we in turn are influenced by the collective consciousness; when the local football team loses, judges give harsher sentences than when they win.[11]

Creativity

It's not just freedom *from* a disorderly functioning brain; Transcendental Meditation also supports the freedom *to* act more creatively. In his book *Super Mind*, Norman Rosenthal suggests that the increase in brainwave coherence found during Transcendental Meditation is at the basis of greater creativity. Rosenthal provides anecdotal stories of increases in creativity, but he also quotes research: a series of three randomized studies on 362 high-school students in Taiwan where the TM group improved compared with controls in terms of fluid intelligence, practical intelligence, trait anxiety, state anxiety, field independence, practical intelligence and creativity; far and away the biggest improvement was in creativity.[12] Commenting on this study, Rosenthal writes:

Besides the credentials of the authors, the prestige of the journal, and the diligence with which the reviewers scoured the data before accepting the manuscript, there are other reasons why I find these findings credible. Over the past decade, I have seen hundreds of TM practitioners (myself included) who have improved – sometimes dramatically – in creativity, field independence and practical intelligence.[13]

The more settled state during Transcendental Meditation

facilitates the ability of the mind to integrate seemingly separate ideas, stimulate the creative process, and come up with new insights. This increase in creativity has been correlated with EEG coherence.[14] Creative ideas often come when we are rested or not directly engaged in purposive activity. An example is the Irish mathematician William Hamilton (1805–65) who had been working on a problem for many years without success, believing he had wasted his time. An insight spontaneously came to him while walking with his wife over a small bridge in Dublin, and although it took more years to articulate it precisely, quaternion functions were born.[15]

Is suffering necessary for creativity? Independent research indicates that there is no difference in the mental health of creative and non-creative people.[16] Maharishi suggests that a person who is suffering will create to escape their pain. But the idea that distress is good for creativity becomes self-defeating, as "in the state of most suffering, life becomes inert; it's a state of non-existence, inertia". When a person is content, 'we are free' to be more creative.[17]

Freedom from economic deprivation

I may be free to travel to another country, but if I do not have much money then how free am I? Having the financial resources could be regarded as having the conditions for liberty. Similarly, a person in a wheelchair is free to walk up the stairs but they do not have the capacity, hence the reason why buildings have ramps for wheelchair access so that theoretical freedom can be made practical.

Increased creativity enables individuals, businesses and national economies to increase their income and wealth, which contributes towards the conditions for freedom. Drs Harald Harung of Norway and Fred Travis of the USA have written about this in their book *Excellence through Mind-Brain Development: The Secrets of World Class Performers*. Research on employees has found reduced burnout, increased productivity and increased cooperation with colleagues as a result of practice of Transcendental Meditation. Companies have introduced TM to employees for two reasons: to promote the well-being of their employees and to increase productivity and profitability for the company. If individuals become more creative, then that greater energy should be reflected in national economic indicators.

There is only one peer-reviewed study on the Maharishi Effect which has its main focus on the economy; thus much fewer than the studies on crime, violence and fatalities. However, if Transcendental Meditation increases creativity in the individual, one would expect there to be a knock-on effect in the economy. A study on Norway and New Zealand, after they had passed the 1% threshold of their respective populations learning Transcendental Meditation, found they advanced more on the International Institute of Management Development's index for national competitive advantage than 34 other industrialized countries.[18] Although the researchers analysed and rejected other possible explanations for the improvement, before we can draw any firm conclusions about the effect of Transcendental Meditation on an economy, more research would be required.

Two case studies

Political freedom is not just the absence of interference and constraints, but is also the ability to have an influence on the rules that govern us and which determine the extent of intrusion and controls in our society. The political theorist Hannah Arendt (1906–75) emphasized new beginnings and the importance of participation; "insert yourself," she would say to her students, "and make the world a little better."[19] Arendt advocates cultivating "creativity, action and responsibility", and the greater confidence and creativity which comes from Transcendental Meditation would further those goals.[20]

The evidence provided so far has been based on quantitative

studies, which produced statistically significant results. There are also two case studies, on Cambodia and Mozambique, which while not as scientific as the quantitative evidence, certainly provide food for thought. In 1993, 15,000 troops in the Mozambique army were taught Transcendental Meditation; this was the initiative of President Joaquim Chissano, who subsequently won the Mo Ibrahim award for good governance. Chissano credits this programme with helping Mozambique transition from a bitter 20-year civil war to peaceful coexistence.[21]

A report from the Development Research Centre at the London School of Economics in 2003 stated: "[Mozambique's] achievements over the last decade are emphasised by the striking contrast with the failed political transition of its twin country, Angola."[22] Angola, which like Mozambique is located in southern Africa, was also a former Portuguese colony and it too had been involved in a civil war which ended around the same time as the war in Mozambique. Whereas Mozambique was able to sustain peace, this was not the case in Angola. Obviously, there can be many reasons for differences in development between two similar nations, but Chissano is convinced of the part played by Transcendental Meditation.

Some evidence for Chissano's perspective is that Mozambique made more progress in holding free and fair elections in the 1990s and early 2000s compared with Angola.[23] Of course the progress with the elections is related to the increased peace, but after President Chissano decided not to stand in the 2004 elections, the drive behind implementing Transcendental Meditation ceased; the meditation tap was in effect turned off. An independent report noted that while Mozambique made "important leaps" in the 1990s and early 2000s, these have not been maintained.[24] Thus, unlike the elections in the 1990s, the 2019 elections in Mozambique were marred by violence and accusations of vote-rigging. Chissano also gives some of the credit for Mozambique's improved economic performance in the

1990s to the implementation of the Transcendental Meditation programme. The research quoted above on New Zealand and Norway lends support to that inference.

Like Chissano, the late King of Cambodia, Norodom Sihanouk, credited Maharishi Vedic University with contributing to the expansion of prosperity in his kingdom.[25] In 1993 in Cambodia, Maharishi encouraged an educational project leading to an increase in the numbers practising Transcendental Meditation and its advanced programmes; it ended in 2008. In 1990 Cambodia was the poorest country of the 42 poorest countries in the world based on income levels. By 2010 Cambodia was ranked 63rd out of 152 on the international scale of poverty, a jump of 89 places in under one generation. In Chapter 3 we briefly referred to a peer-reviewed quantitative study that measured a statistically significant reduction in all violent acts between 1993 and 2008 in Cambodia compared with the baseline period.

An analysis of 193 countries between 1990 and 1998 found that 70 nations changed to a multi-party democracy.[26] Angola was one of nine countries where fighting continued before and after the introduction of multi-party democracy. There were only three countries at war before the transition and peace afterwards: Cambodia, Mozambique and Namibia. While we cannot draw causal conclusions from two case studies, what cannot be disputed is that both Cambodia and Mozambique experienced more political and economic freedom after the introduction of a significant and governmentally approved implementation of Transcendental Meditation. To the extent that such peace-creating groups can contribute to reducing political and economic problems, this will in turn decrease the number of refugees and immigrants seeking a foreign country to improve their quality of life. Chissano, now in his early eighties, is currently working privately to establish an educational project in Mozambique which would include a permanent coherence-creating group.

Chapter 5

The natural tendency of life

Gross national product does not allow for the health of our children…It measures neither our wit nor our courage, neither our wisdom nor our learning, neither our compassion nor our devotion to our country; it measures everything, in short, except that which makes life worthwhile.

Robert F. Kennedy, American politician and lawyer

Bhikhu Parekh, member of the UK House of Lords and former Professor of Political Philosophy, maintains that rights "cannot be the basis of society. Indeed a society that exclusively or even primarily relies on them to define and ensure moral order is too impoverished to nurture valuable forms of human excellence or even to last long."[1] Parekh has claimed that in addition to human rights we need "virtue, responsibility, duty, character and so on". In Chapter 3 we discussed the abolition of slavery, yet the persistence of racial discrimination indicates that something more is needed than just natural or human rights. According to Parekh, it is "the love of goodness". The doctrine of human rights provides a minimal space for the good life; it is then up to us how we fill that space. Certainly, living in a society with established rights is better than living under a totalitarian dictatorship; however, we know that democracies, even with a Bill of Rights, still have problems in spite of established rights; a deeply divided nation may be unable to agree on the content of rights. The thesis of *Healing Social Divisions* is that the 'something more' which makes life worthwhile is the development of higher states of consciousness, the unfolding of human potential. In countries such as Bhutan and New Zealand, there is recognition of the importance of human well-being and happiness, and I would suggest that the information in this chapter would enhance fulfilling those goals.

The cliché of inner happiness

We tend to look to the outside world for our happiness, but it is often claimed that true happiness lies within. Everything in the outside world can change, so it may be thought that we have more control over what happens within ourselves. However, we know that our feelings, emotions and moods can also be quite volatile, so why is it thought that happiness lies within? We could make a mood of happiness, but it would soon be obvious that we are faking it.

Transcendental Meditation is based on the assumption that the mind has a natural tendency to move in the direction of greater happiness. This implies that there is a greater source of happiness within rather than without. Maharishi makes a comparison: "as water flows down a slope, so the mind flows naturally in the direction of bliss."[2] From the perspective of Maharishi's Vedic Science, bliss is a fundamental aspect of life, but whether or not this bliss is experienced depends on the state of balance or imbalance in our physiology. Confirmation of this assertion is found in the research showing decreases in anxiety, improved relationships and increases in self-actualization, and in anecdotal reports from meditators.

Norman Rosenthal asked a group of students who had learned Transcendental Meditation as part of their course at Loyola University's Stritch School of Medicine in Chicago to describe transcendence and received this reply: "stillness, quiet, no boundaries, no thoughts and bliss".[3] One of the students reported: "It was as if someone had opened flood gates and released massive amounts of bliss, joy and harmony."[4] The experience of bliss is particularly striking with the advanced TM programme. Hillary Swanson, a ninth-grade physics and maths teacher in San Diego, California, said: "I feel perfectly calm, and within this silence my bliss is unshakeable. At the same time it takes on a vibrantly energetic quality and I am often moved to laugh with the abandonment of a child."[5]

Now if the state of pure consciousness or Being is beyond experience, how can it be possible to have an experience of happiness in that state? The experience of happiness occurs at the junction point of change and non-change, "when it is on the verge of transcending…at the end of the inward stroke of meditation, and while coming out of transcendence at the start of the outward stroke of meditation".[6]

These inner experiences of bliss have been experienced by people throughout the ages from all cultures. In Chapter 2 we quoted Anwar Sadat writing about "absolute happiness". The American writer Walt Whitman wrote of "The ocean fill'd with joy – the atmosphere all joy!"[7] Plotinus, the founder of Neoplatonism in the third century, said: "If the man that has attained felicity meets some turn of fortune that he would not have chosen, there is not the slightest lessening of his happiness for that."[8] The great German poet Goethe wrote in his poem 'One and All':

How yearns the solitary soul
To melt into the boundless whole,
And find itself again in peace!
The blind desire, the impatient will,
The restless thoughts and plans are still;
We yield ourselves – and wake in bliss.[9]

And Maharishi writes:

The bliss of this state eliminates the possibility of any sorrow, great or small. Into the bright light of the sun no darkness can penetrate; no sorrow can enter bliss consciousness, nor can bliss consciousness know any greater gain than itself.

This state of self-sufficiency leaves one steadfast in oneself, fulfilled in eternal contentment.[10]

Maharishi gained this knowledge from his own experience and the Vedic literature.[11] According to the Vedic tradition, Brahman represents the wholeness of both the changing external aspect of life and the transcendental non-changing aspect. One of the founders of quantum mechanics, Erwin Schrödinger (1887–1961), was impressed by the Upanishads, which is the best-known part of the Vedic literature. This is from the Taittiriya Upanishad:

Having gone within
he recognized that bliss is Brahman.
For truly, out of bliss these beings are born,
in bliss they are sustained
and to bliss they go and merge again.[12]

"Expansion of happiness", writes Maharishi, "is the purpose of life...If a man is unhappy he has missed the very essence of life. If his intelligence, power, creativity and happiness are not constantly developing, he has lost his direction. Life is not meant to be lived in dullness, idleness and suffering; these do not belong to the essential nature of life."[13] This understanding gives substance to the notion of developing happiness from within.

To what extent can a person be completely happy while others in the world are suffering? Do we assume that suffering is an inevitable part of life? It was the contrast between this potential reality of bliss and the actual reality of people suffering in India that motivated Maharishi to leave the Himalayas, where he was living in the mid 1950s, and begin to teach, as it is not necessary for this gap between theory and practice to exist.

Mental rigidities can lead to fear and depression whereas

Transcendental Meditation enlivens bliss. One often reads that love is the basis of happiness in life, but one could also say that a happy person is more able to love. If one is unhappy with one's life it is difficult to be naturally and genuinely giving to another person. Just as the calmness experienced by a sufficient number of people practising Transcendental Meditation translates into reductions in social violence, we would expect increased individual happiness of a significant proportion of the population to translate into a happier and more loving society: to greater social well-being.

Chapter 6

Unity and diversity

Modern enlightened culture is very theory-orientated. We tend to live in our heads, trusting our disengaged understandings: of experience, of beauty...even the ethical: we think that the only valid form of ethical self-direction is through rational maxims or understanding.
Charles Taylor, *A Secular Age*

Glimpses of higher states of consciousness have been found around the world and at different times in history. Maharishi has suggested correlating these experiences with changes in the physiology and more integrated brain functioning in order to remove the development of consciousness from the field of mysticism and place it in the field of scientific investigation.

Dame Jane Goodall, the well-known primatologist, wrote as follows:

> Even the mystics are unable to describe their brief flashes of spiritual ecstasy. It seemed to me, as I struggled afterward to recall the experience, that self was utterly absent: I and the chimpanzees, the earth and the trees and air, seemed to merge, to become one with the spirit power of life itself... Never had I been so intensely aware of the shape, the colour of the individual leaves, the varied patterns of the veins that made each one unique...In a flash of 'outsight' I had known timelessness and quiet ecstasy, sensed a truth of which mainstream science is merely a small fraction.[1]

Goodall recounts an occurrence of unity, but one where the perception of different objects is heightened and more clearly distinguished; the one and the many simultaneously. Maharishi comments on this type of encounter: "Philosophers call this a mystical experience, but it is no more mysterious than is the working of a clock for a child. On one level of consciousness it is normal, on another it is mysterious and again on another it is impossible."[2] Such subjective experiences indicate it may be possible to harmonize opposing values in social life. The physicist Albert Einstein spent the second half of his life attempting to develop a unified field theory and this quest continued after his death in 1955. To what extent these subjective and objective approaches can be harmonized is a question that still remains to be answered.

In Chapter 4, in the discussion on liberty, I suggested that restrictions of freedom have their basis in fear. Maharishi quotes the Upanishads that *certainly fear is born of duality*: "Whenever and wherever there is a sense of two, fear and suffering can exist...The solution lies in the infusion into the field of duality of a non-dual element."[3] The experience of pure consciousness develops unity in the individual and society, which will reduce fear, and this will tend to lead to an increase in freedom. Reductions of anxiety have been measured in those practising Transcendental Meditation and in society.[4]

Harmonizing opposite values

Power needs to be checked but the checks need not take the form of liberal constitutionalism.
Bhikhu Parekh, *Rethinking Multiculturalism*

We all have our different tendencies, likes and dislikes, yet we have to rub along with others. We probably have had the experience that a person who tends to irritate us can behave the same way on a different day and it does not bother us so much; it is like water off a duck's back. When this happens it indicates that our feelings of annoyance are more to do with us than them. If we have slept well, then we have a more positive attitude towards the world, and likewise the deep rest gained during Transcendental Meditation makes life smoother. It is like driving a car with good suspension – we ride the bumps of life more easily. These anecdotal experiences of meditators are backed up by more than 30 studies showing improvements in individual relationships with others as a result of Transcendental Meditation practice. These include but are not limited to less aggressive, irritable and emotionally distant behaviour; and increased sociability, tolerance, capacity for warm interpersonal relationships, emotional and social maturity, empathy, trust and spontaneity.

Can this greater tolerance between individuals be translated into better relations between social groups and different nations? I want to suggest at least four reasons why Transcendental Meditation can help harmonize differences.

1. The 30 studies referred to above suggest greater social harmony on a personal level. Just as violence reduces in both the individual and society, it is not unreasonable to expect improvements in inter-group relations if a sufficient number of people are practising TM; the research we looked at in Chapter 3 provides initial evidence for this assertion.

Development of opposite values through Transcendental Meditation

Faster reaction times	Increased inner calm and tranquillity
Increased autonomy and independence	Increased ability to cooperate with others
Enhanced creativity	Enhanced respect for traditional values
Broader comprehension	Improved ability to focus

	attention
Increased ability to think and act efficiently in the present	Increased foresight
Increased leadership ability, persuasiveness, forcefulness and influence	Decreased tendency to dominate
Increased ego strength	Increased consideration for others
Less tendency to worry about other people's opinions	Greater respect for the views of others
Increased self-sufficiency	Increased capacity for warm interpersonal relationships
Increased enthusiasm for work	Maintenance of a relaxed style of physiological functioning
Increased indications of orderliness of brain functioning	Increased cognitive flexibility
Deep rest in athletes	Improved athletic performance
EEG indications of requirement for less sleep	Improved quality of sleep

2. There is some data on the growth of opposite qualities within the individual, as shown in the table. These developments may be summarized as an integration of opposite styles of physiological functioning. Some of the research studies referred to above were only preliminary, but they provide a direction for future investigation.[5] While we will always have our particular strengths and weaknesses, and our personal preferences, we can develop apparently opposed qualities. Remember these qualities grow spontaneously; those who learn to meditate are not encouraged to develop specific abilities.

3. A general description of the benefit of Transcendental Meditation is more balance in the individual and society.

4. **Singularity and multiplicity.** At a law conference in 1977, Justice V.R.K. Iyer (1915–2014), of the Supreme Court of India, noted that it was an unusual conference bringing together both world-renowned physicists such as E.C.G Sudarshan (1931–2018), who had been nominated six times for a Nobel Prize, and leading legal professionals. According to Iyer:

> This is a conference which deals with the law of laws, of the order behind the orders; and that is where Maharishi comes in. He has a profound grasp of that basis, not of the legal system of country A or country B, the Commonwealth legal system, the British legal system, the American legal system, the Continental legal system – of all these things he is, I hope he will agree, in perfect innocence. But what makes the commonwealth at all? What makes the American legal system? What constitutes the Continental legal system? The projections of the world's legal systems stem from a certain root of which he has got the mastery and the message of this conference will not be how the law of property should be expanded, or how constitutional law should enter new areas of human rights: it will be about *the law of nature which governs all created things* and the law of nature which produces perfect order and punishes those who contravene those laws.[6]
> (Emphasis in the original)

Iyer noted that conventional legal systems work from the outside in, whereas Maharishi's system of natural law works from the inside out. Instead of outside rules it is the creativity of the individual that is developed so that a person spontaneously makes life-supporting choices; Maharishi describes this as acting more in accord with natural law. If individuals are stressed then they will struggle to follow the laws of the land and other social norms. Iyer quoted Justice Cardozo of the United States Supreme Court "that the end of all law is the welfare of society"and this is exactly Maharishi's perspective, but Maharishi traces the source of law beyond legislative bodies[7]. In his response to Justice Iyer's opening remarks, Maharishi gave a summary of his view of the nature of consciousness:

> When we say natural law, we mean the law of evolution... and its nature is awareness, consciousness, intelligence, pure existence which knows itself, pure intelligence. Just because it is consciousness, awareness, it knows itself, and the moment it has the value of knowing itself it has gained the attribute of creative intelligence...It knows itself but the concept of knowing creates duality in that non-dual eternal continuum of unity. This is the first unmanifest sprouting of creative intelligence...It has created within itself, and in this absolute creativity, in the field of the unmanifest, is the seat of all the laws of nature.[8]

Because consciousness is conscious, it can know itself, it is self-referral. This statement contradicts David Hume, Berger and Luckman and many other celebrated thinkers. Readers do not have to take it on trust; in principle you can experience and verify it for yourselves. In knowing itself consciousness becomes three; it becomes what is known, the process of knowing and the knower. There is unity and multiplicity, the one and the many; there is both the diversity of the observer, process of observation and the observed, and the unified state of the three: the opposite values of diversity and singularity. "Here," writes Maharishi, "we have one and three at the same time. When we have one and three together in that self-referral state of pure consciousness, there is that infinite contraction for remaining one and there is that quick expansion to become three. When they are simultaneously three and one there is infinite dynamism."[9] The drawing below provides a schematic view of what is happening when the mind takes an inward turn and settles down to its least excited state.

A schematic representation of the inward turn during Transcendental Meditation

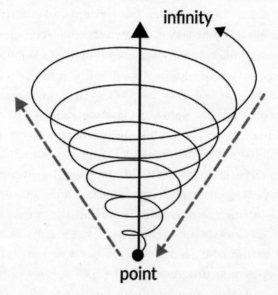

Maharishi described this dynamism as wholeness or silence on the move: "one unbounded ocean of consciousness in motion within itself".[10] At this level of the coexistence of silence and dynamism, every individual point is correlated with every other point; all the individual waves in the ocean are connected at their base. This description of infinity and a point recalls the lines of the English poet William Blake (1757–1827):

To see a World in a Grain of Sand
And a Heaven in a Wild Flower

Hold Infinity in the palm of your hand
And Eternity in an hour

Except that for Maharishi (and probably for Blake too) it is not just fantasy or wish fulfilment but a lived reality:

> Everything is constantly being influenced by everything else. No wave of the ocean is independent of the other. Each certainly has its individuality, but it is not isolated from the influence of the other waves. Every wave has its own course to follow, but this course is dependent on that of every other wave.[11]

We have explained the value of Transcendental Meditation in terms of deep rest allowing accumulated stress in the nervous system to be dissolved. An alternative and equally valid perspective is to understand the benefits in terms of the interplay of silence and dynamism. Thus the alertness experienced during transcending is due to the interaction of silence and dynamism inherent within consciousness. Their coexistence within consciousness gives rise to an evolutionary impulse to grow and progress; it is the basis of our creativity. The process of Transcendental Meditation is one of alternating the attention between unbounded awareness (infinity) during meditation and focused awareness (point) during activity outside of meditation. This same process of point and infinity occurs within meditation when the meditator transcends or goes beyond thought and experiences transcendental consciousness. This relationship between point and infinity may be considered analogous to the particle–wave duality in quantum physics; a subatomic particle is simultaneously localized and spread out. In this way, transcending harmonizes opposite values in the individual and, if there are sufficient numbers, this then has an influence in society and we can measure this in terms of more cooperation between antagonists and reduced fatalities and intensity of war. This harmonizing of opposite values happens without any external coercion and without loss of diversity; in fact as Jane Goodall indicated, diversity is enriched. If permanent coherence groups are established, it will be interesting to see if it is possible to measure the simultaneous and spontaneous increase of harmony and diversity.

Chapter 7

Coherence in collective consciousness: the ground for good governance

Future generations, I suspect, will wonder why it took us so long in the twentieth century to see the centrality of consciousness in the understanding of our very existence as human beings. Why, for so long, did we think that consciousness was unimportant? The paradox is that consciousness is the condition that makes it possible for anything to matter to anybody.
John Searle, *The Mystery of Consciousness*

The American Declaration of Independence states that according to the *Laws of Nature* people are entitled to *certain unalienable Rights...Life, Liberty and the pursuit of Happiness*. To better protect those rights, the US constitution is based on the separation of powers of the legislature, executive and judiciary, a system of checks and balances to prevent the abuse of power by one section of society. No element of society should have absolute power, as power may corrupt, resulting in an infringement of those inalienable rights; neither the president nor anyone else is above the rule of law.

According to Maharishi the system of government is less important than the amount of coherence in collective consciousness. Checks and balances may not be sufficient to prevent an abuse of power. In the USA, if one of the two major parties controls both the executive and the legislature and has also been appointing judges to the judiciary, then the separation of powers is weakened. The institutional checks and balances may need the support of a more orderly collective consciousness. Constitutions may be good on paper but, according to Maharishi, "if the people in the country are disorderly, only the fruit of disorderly action will come to the nation".[1]

The academic subject of political culture studies whether or not the beliefs, norms and values in a nation support the legitimacy of a particular system of government. For example, research has identified the influence of the diverse cultures in the north and south of Italy on the effectiveness of regional government; it has explained this as a variation in "social capital" between the two regions.[2] Social capital refers to trust and cooperation between networks of individuals; this is another way of describing differences in collective consciousness. One problem in this field is how to operationalize or measure the concept of political culture. Surveys of attitudes are essentially descriptive. Maharishi has operationalized the concept of collective consciousness by enabling experimental interventions by varying the numbers practising Transcendental Meditation and then measuring what happens to various objective indicators such as crime and fatalities.

In their book *Transitions to Good Governance: Creating Virtuous Circles of Anti-Corruption*, Dr Alina Mungiu-Pippidi and Professor Michael Johnson trace the process of creating less corrupt governments and societies. They emphasize the importance of the rule of law and note that democracy is no guarantee of an absence of corruption. The task is to go from a system of bribes and favours to "government that can perform basic tasks effectively, credibly and, above all, in ways that are demonstrably fair".[3] The challenge is to change from 'particularism', where bribery, nepotism and patronage are rampant, to ethical universalism, "equal and fair treatment for everyone".[4] More than "political will" is needed to make reforms, and more than activist civil rights groups; movements for reform should also include:

social clubs, ethnic and neighbourhood associations, recreational and hobby groups, and many others whose reasons for being have little immediate connection to the political world...Far from being irrelevant to corruption control, however, they help build networks, teach and diffuse organisational skills, raise levels of social trust and solidarity...and produce legitimate grassroots leadership cadres.[5]

Now that sounds like a move towards a description of collective consciousness. Transcendental Meditation, by enlivening the transcendental level, requires fewer people to be involved to make an impact. With widespread adoption of permanent, larger-than-minimum coherence-creating groups, we would expect to see less corruption and cronyism, and fewer discriminatory laws.

Life is threatened by wars and criminality; liberty can be jeopardized by foreign governments, one's own government and one's fellow citizens; and all of these affect the pursuit of happiness. Reflecting on different systems of government, Maharishi commented:

The fights between different political systems – communism, capitalism, democracy, dictatorship – have occurred because the knowledge of the common feature that binds together all life everywhere, the field of consciousness, has not been available. It is variety that makes a world and it is variety that decorates a world. Different systems of political organisation and social order are like the different-coloured flowers in a flower arrangement. With all its variety of colours the arrangement becomes beautiful. The world was designed to have variety. It is not the differences between political systems that is at fault. What is at fault is the lack of knowledge of the common field of nourishment that gives life to every system everywhere.[6]

This also applies to internal divisions within a society.

Governments should be able to solve problems rather than simply manage them. It is the skills, knowledge and virtue of a people that has the primary influence as to whether there is good governance, rather than the constitution or specific system. The most important resource of any nation is human creativity and intelligence, as that determines how well we use other resources.

Individual choices add up

Law is the mechanics of creation and evolution; it is that binding force which maintains order. Law is that which is order in its structure and function. Law is organizing power. Law is that which guides management and makes management progressive...Law is that which is the basis of everything whether unmanifest wholeness or the expression of unmanifest wholeness – the universe.
Maharishi, *Constitution of India*

In the 1970s, a maximum security prison in Folsom, California, was a pioneer of introducing Transcendental Meditation to prisoners. One of the inmates made the following comment:

A few days ago I was asked for my support in helping a friend kill another man. Even though it was my friend's problem, he knew me for years and was sure he could count on my help. My response to the whole trip was, "I am sorry brother, but it just is not worth it." Even though he understood because we hold a lot of respect for our friendship, I still feel guilty. I had an inner feeling that I was running out on him. My record showed that this was not my style. Through my growth in finding myself through the TM program, I now realize myself, as well as my future, is more important to me than all this madness in prison...I have had many positive experiences since I have been in the TM program, and I feel this is one I will always be proud of. I honestly feel for the first time in 30 years that I can finally take a look at myself, and be comfortable. The TM program has made all this possible without any effort at all.[7]

In this story there is a conflict between loyalty to a friend and committing an act that is morally wrong. The prisoner reduced his stress levels and his brain began to function in a more orderly way, which led to a better decision. Transcendental Meditation does not involve codes of conduct or behavioural guidelines. Changes that occur following practice of TM, whether it is reduced consumption of drugs, less anxiety or better behaviour, happen naturally and spontaneously. Moral insight is gained without moral persuasion. Killing is an obvious example of making the world a more stressful place, but *any* wrong action will create tension in the atmosphere. Maharishi writes:

If one slaps a child in anger, then one has slapped or beaten the whole universe and produced an atmosphere of crying and hatred, suffering and discord – not only in the child but all around him and in the universe. Perhaps the influence of cruelty, hatred, discord and suffering is much greater in the child, and is very faint in the surroundings, but the influence, nonetheless, is there. If every day a majority of people in the world slapped someone and created the same atmosphere, then certainly the intensity of influence of discord, suffering, sorrow and hatred would be enough to show us its effect in the world.[8]

Another example is how our choices affect the environment. When we shop do we use our own reusable bag or do we take plastic bags from the store? Environmental protection requires governmental action, but the individual choices we make also have an influence. Similarly, when we cut down our forests without replanting new trees, it will have ecological consequences. It is the totality of choices we all make every day that determine what sort of world we live in. It is the totality of choices that determine whether the collective consciousness is harmonious or incoherent.

Government is governed by collective consciousness

As long as governments administer society through man-made laws alone, they will never be able to satisfy all the people of the nation. Human intelligence is not sufficiently comprehensive to administer the innumerable trends, tendencies, and values of all the people so that every part of society and the nation as a whole maintains steady, fulfilling progress. Only Nature's intelligence, which perfectly administers the infinite diversity of the universe through Natural Law, is competent to accomplish this.
Maharishi, *Constitution of India*

Governments have to harmonize divisions of wealth, age, gender, religion, culture, ethnicity, class and so on, which may sometimes clash. Creating harmony on the surface is challenging as there are so many features of life which can interact in so many ways and whose consequences are difficult to predict. For example, in economics, forecasting is notoriously difficult. An amusing article in *World Finance* in 2018, by the Canadian mathematician David Orrell, supplies answers (or rather non-answers) to the question from Queen Elizabeth II on her visit to the London School of Economics after the financial crash in 2008: "Why did no one see it coming?"[9] The implication is that something was missing from the analysis of top economists and bankers from around the world. Nobel Prize-winning economist George Akerlof and his co-author Robert Shiller, Professor of Economics at Yale, suggest what the missing element might be: "We will never really understand important economic events unless we confront the fact that their causes are largely mental in nature."[10] In chapter one of their book *Animal Spirits: How Human Psychology Drives the Economy, and Why It Matters for Global Capitalism*, they write about collective confidence. Other research on 40 countries provides evidence that national mood influences stock returns.[11] While these economists deserve credit for highlighting the importance of human consciousness, there is not a clear understanding of collective consciousness.

I have provided evidence that a consciousness-based approach to improving society will reduce fatalities, and increase freedom and happiness. In the Davies and Alexander study referred to in Chapter 3, the expert coder who was blind to the purpose of the research measured an increase in cooperation between antagonists who were trying to kill each other. Neutralizing stress in the collective consciousness creates more harmony in society and it is predicted that governments will make better decisions. The implication of this is that we can all contribute to influencing the quality of life and the quality of governance in our country. Instead of blaming the government for social problems, we can all take responsibility to create more harmony in the collective consciousness. "All problems of government", writes Maharishi, "result from the violation of Natural Law by the whole population, which leads to stress in collective consciousness. Accumulated stress inevitably erupts in problems and disorderly behaviour in society."[12] By violation of natural law, Maharishi means when our behaviour is inappropriate (whether murder or a slap); when our actions are more life-supporting, this is acting in accord with the laws of nature. From a scientific perspective everything we do, whether good or bad, is in accord with the laws of nature. Maharishi is referring to the consequences of our actions for the well-being of oneself, those around us and the whole environment. For example, the careless use of plastics, which can take thousands of years to decay, has resulted in much of it ending up in our oceans, harming marine life, entering into the human food chain and ultimately harming ourselves.

It is not simply a fortunate coincidence that there is a relationship between collective consciousness and liberty, happiness and social harmony; they are all qualities intrinsic to the least excited state of consciousness. In the previous chapter we discussed the interaction of dynamism and silence which Maharishi described as wholeness moving within itself, and he says this initial delicate activity is the origin of law in nature. Thus the coexistence of dynamism and silence in the least excited state of consciousness gives life an impulse to evolve. The specific way this impulse manifests in human society depends on all the thoughts, speech and behaviour of everyone who makes up the world. While this may seem abstract, the peer-reviewed evidence and the direct experience of meditators supports the perspective that the amount of coherence in collective consciousness influences the quality of governance; if a government is not able to prevent violence and reduce crime, these will interfere with good governance.

Excess stress (as opposed to stimulation and challenge) can be thought of as creating imbalance or disorder. When we transcend and neutralize stress we are restoring order both to our own body and mind and to the communities in which we participate, from the family, through the local community, the region, the nation and the entire world. Violation of natural law creates stress; stress in the nervous system makes it more difficult to act in accord with natural law; transcending enables a person to break out of this cycle by creating more orderliness in brain functioning. It is as if we start to swim with the current of life rather than swimming against it. Life becomes less of a struggle for the individual and potentially for society. Increased coherence in collective consciousness creates more social harmony. Maharishi explains this in terms of individuals and society as a whole acting more in accord with the laws of nature, as Maharishi regards our own least excited state of consciousness as the home or source of all the laws of nature:

National consciousness governs the activity of every nation in the same way that the consciousness of the individual governs the activity of the individual. Since national consciousness is the collective consciousness of all the individuals of the nation, it is ultimately the consciousness of the individual that is the prime mover of the nation and shapes its destiny... Therefore it is the prime duty of the ruler of the nation to maintain coherence in national consciousness, and this is easy to do by maintaining a coherence-creating group and by providing proper education.[13]

By proper education, Maharishi means the inclusion of the development of consciousness in addition to the conventional subjects.

Twelve principles of good governance

The Council of Europe, which is made up of 47 European nations, and is a separate and distinct organization from the European Union, outlined 12 principles of good governance in 2008, as follows:

1. Fair conduct of elections, representation and participation
2. Responsiveness
3. Efficiency and effectiveness
4. Openness and transparency
5. Rule of law
6. Ethical conduct
7. Competence and capacity
8. Innovation and openness to change
9. Sustainability and long-term orientation
10. Sound financial management
11. Human rights, cultural diversity and social cohesion
12. Accountability

All of these principles have their roots in human consciousness, and without creating more coherence in collective consciousness these laudable goals will be limited in their fulfilment. There are at least four barriers that have to be overcome: narrowness of vision, short-termism, competing interests and failures of implementation.[14] *Healing Social Divisions* highlights a body of research which, by enlivening collective consciousness in a more orderly direction, can contribute to overcoming these barriers and achieving these aims.

The educational perspective referred to in the quote at the end of the previous section is that unfolding our full human potential leads to action which is more in accord with natural law. We may not know the laws of nature or codes of conduct intellectually, but when we act, after having infused more pure consciousness into our mind, we will, like the prison inmates who learn Transcendental Meditation, make fewer mistakes. Maharishi provides an account of behaviour on the basis of the aphorism, *as you sow so shall you reap*; if you eat bad food you will become ill; if factories pollute the air there will be an increase in respiratory illnesses. Whether we act in accord with the laws of nature or choose to violate laws of nature, there are repercussions. Often we know that what we are doing is probably not right, but sometimes we still do it anyway. Intellectual knowledge of right and wrong is insufficient; we need to raise our level of consciousness so that we spontaneously act in accord with natural law. In the discussion with Matti Golan, Maharishi was explaining that when relatively few people create more coherence in the collective consciousness, attitudes will change and the actions of the government will transform in the direction of better governance and this can be measured.

The 12 principles above are incomplete. They do not cover what functions should be carried out by central government and which by local government; how much of social life should be carried out by the state and how much by the private sector working for profit and how much by non-profit organizations. The quote from Maharishi at the start of the previous section maintains that "human intelligence is not sufficiently comprehensive" to resolve complex issues of governmental administration. His solution to human incompleteness of knowledge is to harness the intelligence of nature through citizens acting more in accord with natural law.[15] At the moment there is not sufficient peer-reviewed evidence to know if this is correct, but we do know that use of reason and dialogue alone has not solved these age-old problems of governance and that enlivening consciousness promotes balance and integration, so it is not an unreasonable hypothesis.

General will and the spirit of the people

But laws can't be enacted or sustained without the hearts and minds of people.
Martha C. Nussbaum, *The Monarchy of Fear*

The Genevan philosopher Jean-Jacques Rousseau (1712–78) formed a concept of the general will, the idea that it is the people who ultimately make the laws. This is different from collective consciousness. Collective consciousness is the background social atmosphere made up from all the individuals, and this determines the level of coherence or harmony in a society. The general will could suffer from the same problem as the tyranny of the majority in a democracy; it could pass a law that discriminated against a minority without any good justification. Rousseau has gained notoriety for his statement: "Whoever refuses to obey the general will, will be forced to do so by the entire body; this means merely that he will be forced to be free."[16] If you are being forced you are not free.

Another related concept is *Volksgeist* or 'spirit of the people', that each nation will have its own specific national character.

This may be thought of as a precursor to Durkheim's idea of collective consciousness. Durkheim advocated conventional education to instil moral values; while accepting the need to educate people in the traditional values of a society, Maharishi placed more emphasis on the expansion of consciousness, as that will have a greater influence in creating a more orderly and harmonious collective consciousness.

Variety is the stuff of relative life

Even having created maximum coherence in the collective consciousness, there would still be differences of opinion on how best to organize society. "Even remaining within the range of happiness," writes Maharishi, "life could be lived in many different ways. Even when every man on earth is using his full potential, all men would not be the same."[17] This would be the case whether we are referring to individuals or whole cultures. Dr Vernon Katz writes: "It is wrong, if very human, to seek the unchanging values of the absolute in the flux of the relative. I may not yet be secure in the absoluteness of the Absolute but Maharishi has certainly taught me the relativity of things relative."[18] Katz also relates how Maharishi was always fresh in his approach, there was nothing formulaic or preconceived; he was always in the present, as if everything was new; he was not working on the level of memory: "I realised that Maharishi does not recall: he recreates."[19] The following emphasizes this point about differences:

Nature loves variety. World harmony is not based on the fusion of different cultures. It depends on the ability of each culture to maintain its own integrity on the basis of the infinite adaptability that characterises life lived in accord with the laws of nature. Like the many-coloured pieces of a mosaic or the varied tunes of an orchestra, each fully integrated culture contributes to form a harmonious world.[20]

The health and happiness of all citizens and non-citizens should be at the heart of politics; we need to develop *a culture of civility*.[21] The research on Transcendental Meditation as a whole indicates that taxpayers' money could be saved if there was widespread use of this peace-creating technology. The research provides evidence that permanent coherence-creating groups would support the achievement of government policy: more harmonious international relations, economic development, reducing all kinds of violence, and decreasing crime and motor accidents.[22] Huw Dixon, Professor of Economics at Cardiff University, supports this perspective: "There is now a strong and coherent body of evidence showing that [this approach] provides a simple and cost-effective solution to many of the social problems we face today. This research and its conclusions are so strong, that it demands action from those responsible for government policy."[23]

Chapter 8

A paradigm of connectivity

The real problem of humanity is the following: we have paleolithic emotions; medieval institutions; and god-like technology. And it is terrifically dangerous, and it is now approaching a point of crisis overall...until we answer those huge questions of philosophy that the philosophers abandoned a couple of generations ago – Where do we come from? Who are we? Where are we going? – rationally, we're on very thin ground.
E.O. Wilson, American sociobiologist

The conventional wisdom about the relationship of mind and body is that consciousness is a by-product or epiphenomenon of the functioning of the brain and nervous system; consciousness is an emergent property, having its basis in matter. The causality is one way; matter influences consciousness, but consciousness has no causal impact on matter. The research on different kinds of meditation suggests that mental techniques of meditation can influence the body in a variety of ways. Research by Sara Lazar at Harvard has found that Buddhist Insight meditation leads to increased cortical thickness.[1] In Transcendental Meditation, greater EEG brainwave coherence or synchrony is found all over the brain and especially in the prefrontal cortex. Recent research has found that talking therapies such as Cognitive Behavioural Therapy are not just psychological but have a physical influence on the brain.[2] In recent years the placebo effect has been investigated more closely and it seems that a patient's expectations will influence the effect of medicine they take, whether or not the *medicine* contains any active ingredients.[3]

This suggests that the causal influence between mind and body is in both directions. For the ordinary person, this is not difficult to comprehend; I have an idea to raise my arm and up it goes. But how is it that body and consciousness interact? One can understand matter influencing matter, for example two billiard balls hitting each other; one can understand mental phenomena influencing mental phenomena, a mother's love for her child producing an effect. Mind–body interactions raise problems of precisely how they work together.

At any one time we have a body of knowledge and we have theories to explain how it all hangs together. Sometimes new scientific findings emerge that question the existing paradigm of how things work. The research on all types of meditation, on talking therapies, on the placebo effect, challenge the current understanding of the relationship between mind and body. There are many organizations, as well as respected scientists and doctors around the world, who are questioning this traditional paradigm.[4] No longer can we categorically say that the mind does not have a real influence on the body. This is not an especially shocking revelation. However, the thesis of *Healing Social Divisions* goes much further than saying that mind and meditation can influence bodily functioning. We have referred to research, based on 50 demonstrations and 150 outcomes, showing that the practice of Transcendental Meditation and its advanced programmes by a relatively small proportion of the population will influence the behaviour of others without any direct interaction or contact between them. This challenges the idea of an atomistic world where we are all separate from each other, that consciousness is confined within our bodies and has no causal efficacy. There are at least three responses to these research findings:

1. The interpretation of the data must be flawed and there are more conventional explanations for decreases in political violence, crime, car accidents and so on, other than creating more coherence or orderliness in collective

consciousness.

2. The interpretation of the data is correct and we need to take a radically different view of human consciousness and how we are connected with each other.
3. Interesting – let's do some more research.

The problem with the first position is that we may be missing out on a relatively simple way to solve many social issues, and in terms of government expenditure the cost of testing these proposals is insignificant. The problem with the second position is we have to accept not only that the mind has an influence on the body but that it has influence on others without direct interaction; I cannot have an idea to raise *your* arm and your arm goes up unless I use force. The idea that meditation can influence another person at a distance seems to fit Einstein's description of *spooky action at a distance*. Yet the empirical evidence seems to suggest that social violence does decrease when a sufficient number of people are practising Transcendental Meditation; it is a way to increase the orderliness or harmony in collective consciousness and then measure the effects. This has huge potential, so let's have some independent research from governments.

Matter and consciousness

Although the classical philosophies of India, China and Greece differ in important ways, there are some highly important commonalities. Each started with a basic assumption that everything is one.
Julian Baggini, *How the World Thinks*

In Chapter 3 I asked how Maharishi knew that transcending could have this influence on decreasing negative social trends; it was derived from his interpretation of Yoga and Vedanta, two of the six systems of Indian Philosophy. Traditionally

115

these systems have been regarded as being in competition with each other. Maharishi says this is a misunderstanding and sees the six systems as part of one holistic understanding. The title of a recent book by Dr Tony Nader, *One Unbounded Ocean of Consciousness*, gives Maharishi's point of view: we live in an interconnected world with both unity and multiplicity, but the fundamental reality is consciousness rather than matter (see the Appendix). Maharishi describes the least excited state of consciousness as the home of all the laws of nature. Similar views have been proposed throughout the ages and in many cultures. Aldous Huxley described this view as the 'perennial philosophy' and it has taken both secular and religious forms. This perspective is not restricted to the East; while at the University of Michigan, the philosopher David Skrbina wrote about this tradition in the West, from the ancient Greeks to modern scientists and philosophers. For example, Sir Arthur Eddington (1882–1944), the British physicist who confirmed the predictions of Einstein's general theory of relativity, said: "the stuff of the world is mind-stuff."[5] A subatomic particle, rather than being like a tiny billiard ball, is more accurately described as an abstract wave, a bundle of energy; an abstract conceptual entity. Nobel Laureate and mathematical physicist Sir Roger Penrose says: "Would one still want to call a world-view 'physics-based' if it contains elements of protomentality at a basic level? This is a matter of terminology, but it is one that I am reasonably happy with for the moment at least."[6]

Nobel Laureate Erwin Schrödinger, the quantum physicist famous for both the equation and the cat named after him, commented on Huxley's *Perennial Philosophy*:

Still, it must be said that to Western thought this doctrine has little appeal, it is unpalatable, it is dubbed fantastic, unscientific. Well, so it is because our science – Greek science – is based on objectivation, whereby it has cut itself off from an adequate understanding of the Subject of Cognizance, of the mind. But I do believe that this is precisely the point where our present way of thinking does need to be amended, perhaps by a bit of blood-transfusion from Eastern thought. That will not be easy, we must beware of blunders – blood-transfusion always needs great precaution to prevent clotting. We do not wish to lose the logical precision that our scientific thought has reached, and that is unparalleled anywhere at any epoch.[7]

These three distinguished physicists assert that an expanded concept of consciousness is fundamental to understanding our world; more physicists and mathematicians who share this view are listed in the endnotes.[8] While the personal views of particular physicists and mathematicians do not constitute any form of proof, they certainly show that this perspective is not unreasonable. Neither does the perennial philosophy constitute a proof. However, the fact that so far the peer-reviewed statistical research has tended to confirm Maharishi's predictions regarding the influence of Transcendental Meditation should provide confidence that this consciousness-based approach to solving social problems is worth further exploration. While we do not yet have a complete scientific understanding of this phenomenon, progress in quantum biology and the possibility of quantum coherence in the brain may help to shed light on the mechanisms of the Maharishi Effect.[9]

Subjective perspectives

If the doors of perception were cleansed every thing would appear to man as it is, Infinite. For man has closed himself up, till he sees all things thro' narrow chinks of his cavern.
William Blake, *Marriage of Heaven and Hell*

Personal experiences of those adopting Maharishi's programmes provide a subjective validation of objective empirical research. Here are some experiences from teachers of Transcendental Meditation on an extended meditation retreat:

> Boundless infinitude, beautiful bliss, total silence. In activity a powerful silent wholeness rests on the surface of everything. A beautiful softness connects and inter-fuses all I see.[10]

> I would see the object and know it to be myself. A few examples are: I saw the stars, planets, and galaxies of the universe spread out before me and instantly knew them to be part of myself – the same sense of recognition one experiences when one sees unexpectedly one's image reflected in a mirror.[11]

> During meditation the experiences of being the whole universe started to occur more and more often...Outside meditation my heart has been expanding so incredibly. I feel like I have been encompassing everything with the love and bliss that have been growing so greatly and rapidly.[12]

> A very nice change which has taken place is an unbroken intimacy between my Self and the environment.[13]

Experiences such as these have been recorded in many cultures throughout recorded history. The idea that when we are at peace with ourselves we will be at peace with others is well expressed by the Sioux medicine man Black Elk (1862–1950). He refers to *Wakan-Tanka*, which can be translated as *the Great Spirit*, and refers to one's real Self and to an unmanifest, all-pervading field of intelligence that both created and is embodied in the universe:

> The first peace, which is the most important, is that which

comes within the soul of men when they realize their relationship, their oneness, with the universe and all its powers, and when they realize that at the centre of the universe dwells *Wakan-Tanka* and that this centre is really everywhere, it is within each of us. This is the real Peace, and the others are but reflections of this. The second peace is that which is made between two individuals, and the third is that which is made between two nations. But above all you should understand that there can never be peace between nations until there is first known that true peace which, as I have often said, is within the souls of men.[14]

In the Zen tradition, a pictorial story depicts ten stages of a young ox-herder searching for and finding fulfilment within himself, becoming more compassionate, connected to society and wanting to help relieve suffering.[15]

For those who have not had the experience of transcendental consciousness, the ideas in *Healing Social Divisions* are theoretical and perhaps a little dry. Once one has had the experience, they become more alive and believable. It is a little like trying to describe the taste of a strawberry to someone who has never eaten one; at some point one just has to try it for oneself. It is this enlivenment of inner bliss in the individual which influences the collective consciousness and which can heal social divisions.

Transcendental Meditation has been subject to empirical research and there is no reason why there cannot be larger and more rigorous studies undertaken. Non-meditating academics are taking more interest in researching Transcendental Meditation; here is a comment from a peer reviewer of Maharishi Effect research:

In short, the evidence presented is of the type that I would call a 'prima facie' convincing argument. Hence the author is left with the problem that the hypothesis falls outside the normal peace research/conflict studies paradigm and paradigms are difficult to budge...It's possible that people's auto accidents and fire and burglaries are influenced by the social environments around them. Days that are more stressful, people are less cautious in traffic and they have more traffic accidents or they leave the iron on or whatever else. So, I'm willing to believe that the social environment around can influence those behaviors...That's actually where the research gives me much harder problems than the conflict. It's the little stuff.[16]

In many academic disciplines there is a realization that consciousness has been neglected; Transcendental Meditation provides a universal method for operationalizing both individual and collective consciousness. The paradigm suggested by Maharishi from the tradition of Vedanta is one that bears similarities to the traditional wisdom of humankind found in many diverse cultures. Finally, one can experience pure consciousness and its growth for oneself.

Chapter 9

How to love your neighbour and your environment as yourself

Reason has already made as strong a case as reason can and it is clear now that pure reason or argument alone does not mobilise change. Nor do we need more blueprints for an ecological society. Blueprints do not in themselves, as it turns out, bring about change, any more than philosophical arguments do. Nor does science. Existing environmental sciences, incomplete as they admittedly are, are already pointing to a planet ecologically in extremis. Yet this is not triggering a corresponding awakening except insofar as ecological extremis places humanity in jeopardy.

Freya Mathews, *We've had forty years of environmental ethics – and the world is getting worse*

When Joe Biden was inaugurated as US President on 20 January 2021 he said: "There is truth and there are lies told for power and profit...each of us has a duty and responsibility to defend the truth and to defeat the lies."[1] One of my motivations in writing this book is the outrageous telling of lies in public – lies which some, with a straight face, have called alternative facts. Lying in politics is as old as recorded history, and some recent research in Spain found that those mayors with a greater propensity to lie were more likely to be re-elected, so it is no surprise that politicians tell lies.[2] While the occasional liar may take their lies with them to their grave, systematic lying will eventually run up against the *stubbornness of facts*.[3] In the long term, lies will lead to inefficiencies in practical affairs; in the short term they cause disorder and division. "Politicians who tell lies erode democracy, damage society and hurt us all," says a recent book that offers some practical solutions to the problem.[4] By this stage of *Healing Social Divisions* you will not be surprised to hear that the root of this problem is a lack of coherence in collective consciousness.

I want to consider why Transcendental Meditation may contribute to creating a society where truth is more highly valued.

1. While lying and criminality are not the same, they overlap; in both cases other people are being treated as means rather than as ends in themselves. We have seen evidence that Transcendental Meditation can reduce recidivism, the rate at which previous inmates return to prison. This suggests an increase in honesty on an individual level. There has also been some preliminary research on improved moral maturity in those practising TM compared with controls and it has shown that improved moral reasoning has been correlated with more integrated brain functioning as measured by EEG.[5]

2. If our sense of self, of who we are, is derived from the experience of pure consciousness rather than our beliefs, attributes or possessions, we are more likely to appreciate different perspectives instead of being attached to our own convictions irrespective of the evidence.

3. The development of self-actualization and higher states of consciousness increases the ability to view people in a more loving manner; to treat people as ends in themselves rather than as merely instrumental in satisfying our own needs. We are less likely to regard them as the *other* but will grow in the ability to *love our neighbour as our self*.

4. The least excited state of consciousness is described in the Vedic tradition as *Sat-Chit-Ananda*, which can be translated as truth, consciousness and bliss. *Sat* means truth or that which does not change. One common report

122

of people learning Transcendental Meditation is a feeling of increased stability or being more centred yet at the same time being better able to adapt to changing circumstances. They no longer feel like a football being kicked around by external circumstances. It is the quality of non-change becoming livelier in everyday activity that is the basis for this greater stability and adaptability. The growth of field independence through Transcendental Meditation is evidence of stability, and increased creativity is evidence for greater ability to adapt. This provides a foundation for activity in terms of increasing physiological, psychological, sociological and ecological stability. If there were permanent coherence-creating groups around the world, would nations value truth to a greater extent than in contemporary social life? Would it help to bridge the separation between truth and politics?

Truth, liberty, happiness and harmony are not superficial add-ons to life but are inherent in the nature of the least excited state of consciousness, and it is our choice how much those values express themselves in our life; it can be more or less. The state of least excitation is a state of non-change, and non-change is the essence of truth. I would expect the widespread use of coherence-creating groups to lead to an increase in the values of truth, life, liberty and happiness which often seem to have gone absent without leave in our world. Fulfilment is found by first taking an inward turn to locate the abstract field of Being and then, established in that, by performing action in life, which will meet with more success than would otherwise have been the case. This is not wishful thinking but is based on empirical evidence, and it is always possible to undertake more research.

Enlarging our moral circle

What is the moral significance, if any, of national borders? Do we owe more to our fellow citizens than we owe citizens of other countries? In a global age, should we cultivate national identities or should we aspire to a cosmopolitan ethic of universal human concern?
Michael Sandel, *Populism, Liberalism and Democracy*

Who is part of our moral circle; who is and who is not the *other*; who or what is of greater or lesser value and to what extent can we interact with them? The growth of higher states of consciousness enlarges our moral circle but without sacrificing our individuality or cultural traditions. It enables us to treat all people and the environment as ends in themselves and not merely as a means to an end. The issue of social divisions is seeing people as foreign to us, whether it is due to nationality, ethnicity, race, gender, age, culture and so on; seeing them as the *other*. The solution, according to Maharishi, is the experience of pure consciousness or Being by a sufficient number of the population of a society. Maharishi explains as follows:

the Transcendental Meditation technique effortlessly takes the individual's mind to that area of unbounded awareness which is the source of all thinking and is the home of all the laws of nature. At this level of unbounded consciousness all the myriad levels of separate elements which make up natural law are constantly and very intimately linked together, because unbounded awareness is an area of infinite correlation. This means there is such togetherness and each separate element is so close to the other that it is the other.[6]

We can make an analogy; a human nervous system with

less stress is like a radio receiver picking up a signal with minimal or no interference, and the resulting clear broadcast is equivalent to action in accord with natural law. A stressed person will not have such clear experiences of unbounded awareness and thus is more likely to violate laws of nature, that is behave in a way that will create suffering and problems for themselves and their environment. The restful alertness experienced in Transcendental Meditation neutralizes stress so that one is more in tune with what Maharishi describes as the home of all the laws of nature. One adjusts the dial on the radio for a clearer reception and a signal which is less noisy and distorted. In effect, "the individual can consciously place himself in this eternally evolving stream of nature, thereby allowing himself to be carried forward by the natural flow of cosmic evolution".[7]

Similarly, a society or country can put itself in this evolving stream of nature; Maharishi describes this as national law being in accord with natural law:

Imbalance in nature merely means lack of co-ordination among its various separate elements...When the value of infinite correlation is not enlivened, then it is as if correlation were frozen. Inertia reigns. Communication is frozen and there is lack of co-ordination. The result is chaotic happenings and imbalance in nature.[8]

When it is enlivened, there is a move towards a frictionless flow of communication and it becomes possible for long-standing disputes which seemed to be insoluble to find resolution. In Chapter 7 I highlighted the limitations of human intelligence, and the need is for a broadened, more all-encompassing awareness for healing social divisions.

A related idea can be found in the writings of Norwegian ecologist Arne Naess (1912–2009) who said we need to expand our conception of self from a narrow egoistic self to an expanded ecological self which includes all of the earth's living systems. He attributes environmental degradation to a narrowness of vision; we need to begin to view the world around us as an extension of ourselves rather than as something separate; but this extension needs to be more than intellectual imagination – it has to be a lived reality. Writing about *Panpsychism in the West*, the idea that all things have a mind or mind-like quality, the philosopher David Skrbina writes:

> The great irony, of course, is that in harming nature we harm ourselves. As we deplete the soil, deforest the land, exterminate species, exhaust the seas and warm the planet we pay a high and growing price...All this suggests that our mechanistic world view is in error; that, by treating nature as mindless, we engage in irrational and destructive behaviour. Metaphysics has consequences.[9]

Narrowness of vision is not only a problem for the environment but also creates problems in our systems of health, education, rehabilitation, national defence and systems of government. It is important to put life, health and happiness ahead of short-term profits. Emphasis should be on the prevention of problems rather than cleaning up the mess after the event. The establishment of permanent groups, whose profession it is to create greater harmony, orderliness and coherence in collective consciousness, will contribute to creating more balance and progress in all areas of life. The result is an expansion of consciousness, the enlargement of our moral circle; hence the saying, *the world is my family*. A person may have multiple identities: the place where they grow up, the region, their religion, their ethnicity, their hobbies, the nation, the continent and the world.

Enlarging the moral circle

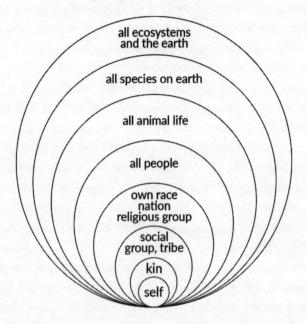

This understanding of the primacy of consciousness does not undermine other approaches to changing society; rather it adds an extra layer which can contribute to a deeper appreciation of the mechanics of social change. Durkheim was ahead of his time in writing about the collective consciousness with a life of its own. There have been many attempts to understand the relationship between the individual and the collective aspects of society. There are traditional theories such as communism, socialism, liberalism, neoliberalism and capitalism, and more recent ones, including but not limited to pluralism, imagined communities, enlarged mentality, communicative action, political theology, multiculturalism, trans-nationalism and trans-individuality. At the start of Chapter 2 I referred to Lyotard's call for micro-narratives to replace grand narratives such as democracy and Marxism. This consciousness-based approach to healing social divisions starts with the individual and, with a sufficient number of individuals, has an influence on the whole society; thus it is simultaneously a micro and a grand narrative. A more expanded concept of consciousness does not contradict traditional political theories but adds an additional level of consideration.

A current practical problem is large global corporations that legally avoid paying much tax compared with companies that operate within a particular country. In principle, solving this problem is not difficult; as I complete the manuscript of this book in May 2021, cooperation between nation states on this issue is starting to happen. Similarly, the problem of high tech and social media companies harvesting the data of billions of people and the misuse of social media platforms requires nation states to work together; creating more coherence in collective consciousness would facilitate progress towards accomplishing these goals. Many problems faced by the world are global in nature – crime, pandemics, environmental issues, biological weapons – and require international cooperation.

In 2015 the United Nations agreed on 17 sustainable development goals. It is one thing to have goals; it is another for them to be fulfilled in practice. There is much research on the effect of Transcendental Meditation in improving health and education outcomes, plus some preliminary data about economic development both for the individual and society. Regarding the other goals, if the development of consciousness enlivens balance, dynamism and orderliness in society as a whole, then one can begin to see how that might influence the attainment of these laudable aims. The key assumption is that transcendental consciousness is at the basis of all thinking, achievement and fulfilment; and we don't have to assume or rely on hope; the possibility of creating a more enlightened civilization can be tested.

Conclusion

What is intelligible, even true, may not be easy to believe.
Alyssa Ney, *The World in the Wave Function: A Metaphysics for Quantum Physics*

The experience of pure consciousness offers a practical and knowledge-based approach to healing social divisions. Establishing permanent coherence-creating groups of people practising the advanced Transcendental Meditation programme does not invalidate conventional methods of creating a better world; it would support and enhance the success of those efforts. Change will come through existing mechanisms and institutions, but such transformations would occur more quickly. Dr Juan Pascual-Leone, Professor Emeritus at York University in Ottawa, Canada, who familiarized himself with the studies on the Maharishi Effect, commented: "The possibility is that we have made one of the most important discoveries of our time."[10] I would like to give the final word to the German philosopher Arthur Schopenhauer (1788–1860) from his book *The World as*

Will and Representation: *"All truth passes through three stages. First, it is ridiculed. Second, it is violently opposed. Third, it is accepted as being self-evident."*

Appendix

Knowledge is different in different states of consciousness

Consciousness is not a thing among things; it is the horizon that contains everything.
Edmund Husserl, German philosopher

This research [on the Maharishi Effect] is exciting. It is a non-traditional conception, but the straightforward evidence gives the theory credence in my eyes.
Ved Nanda, PhD, director of the International Legal Studies Program, University of Denver

We see the sun rise and set but know that the earth spins on its axis as it rotates around the sun. This was confirmed by the telescope, which extended our knowledge of the outer world. Transcendental Meditation extends our knowledge of consciousness and allows us to derive testable hypotheses. Transcending expands consciousness, resulting in stress being neutralized, and this influences our perception and behaviour.

In 1963, Maharishi wrote his first book, *The Science of Being and Art of Living*. Early on he refers to the attempts by Albert Einstein to establish scientifically the unified field theory:

Einstein seems to have been clearly aware of the possibility of one basis for all diversity, one common denominator for all the multiplicity of creation. He was at least trying to establish one constant at the basis of all relative existence. If physical science should arrive at the conclusion which Einstein was trying to pinpoint with his unified field theory, one constant

131

would be established as the basis of all relative creation.[1]

If and when physics develops a unified understanding of the four fundamental forces of nature and how they interact, Maharishi suggested that:

> This will serve to turn the world of physical science towards the science of mental phenomena. Theories of mind, intellect, and ego will supersede the findings of physical science. At the ultimate or the extreme limit of investigation into the nature of reality in the field of the mind will eventually be located the state of pure consciousness, that field of the transcendental nature lying beyond all relative existence of material and mental values of life.[2]

Maharishi is not alone in thinking that consciousness is fundamental to the world in which we live. This understanding explains why enlivening the least excited state of consciousness would have a wide influence on the individual and society. Maharishi, who had studied physics himself at university, kept up to date with the developments in unified field theory, from super gravity to string theory and M theory. In the 1980s Maharishi worked with scientists in various disciplines to develop a series of Unified Field Charts. These are a graphic representation of the principle that *knowledge is structured in consciousness*; that all knowledge has its basis in consciousness. While pictures and words cannot completely capture ideas that are beyond space and language, the chart below may provide some insight. It is a simplified version of the unified field chart for physics and gives a schematic representation of Maharishi's understanding about the relationship of matter and consciousness. More complete versions can be found on the internet if you search for Unified Field Charts under 'images'.

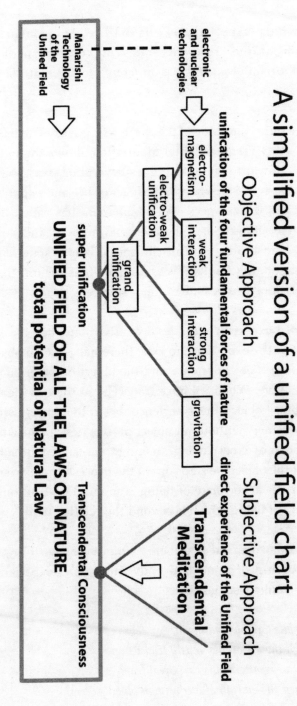

A simplified version of a unified field chart

Objective Approach
unification of the four fundamental forces of nature

Subjective Approach
direct experience of the Unified Field

electronic
and nuclear
technologies

electro-
magnetism

electro-weak
unification

weak
interaction

grand
unification

strong
interaction

gravitation

Transcendental
Meditation

Maharishi
Technology
of the
Unified Field

super unification

Transcendental Consciousness

UNIFIED FIELD OF ALL THE LAWS OF NATURE
total potential of Natural Law

The following perspectives on this chart relate to Maharishi's description of the different states of consciousness and to the aphorism, *knowledge is different in different states of consciousness.*

1. On the right-hand side of the chart, where it says "subjective approach", Transcendental Meditation allows the mind to take an inward turn until it goes beyond or transcends the finest aspect of the changing aspect of life and experiences a non-changing aspect which Maharishi has called Being, pure consciousness, unbounded awareness and in this chart Transcendental Consciousness. It is a state of Self-realization. In Chapter 2 we described it as the fourth state of consciousness, a state of inner silence.

The word experience implies a relative state; it is a relative word. For the experience to exist there has to be an object of experience. The experience and the object of experience are both relative. When we have transcended the experience of the subtlest object, the experiencer is left by himself without an experience, without an object of experience and without the process of experiencing...having transcended the subtlest state of the object, he steps out of the process of experiencing and arrives at the state of Being. The mind is then found in the state of Being which is beyond the relative field.[3]

Again Wordsworth, in his poem 'Tintern Abbey', brings out the relationship of mind and body during the experience of transcendental consciousness:

that serene and blessed mood,
In which the affections gently lead us on, –
Until, the breath of this corporeal frame
And even the motion of our human blood

Almost suspended, we are laid asleep
In body, and become a living soul...

The left-hand side of the chart represents objective material existence and could be equated with waking, dreaming and sleep states of consciousness. In this instance the chart shows physics, but it could be applied to any area of life.

2. Another way to look at the chart is to see it in two halves: below and above the horizontal line; below represents the non-changing aspect, and above represents change. Cosmic consciousness, the fifth state of consciousness, is described as living these two values simultaneously. The advanced programme of Transcendental Meditation, known as the TM-Sidhi programme, enhances the development of cosmic consciousness by developing the ability to maintain silence in the midst of activity. Schematically we can think of the horizontal line as a junction point between change and non-change and it is at this level that the TM-Sidhi techniques are used. We would then be living the full value of inner and outer life; it is a state of inner stability where a person is able to cope with the vicissitudes of outer life.

3. In Chapter 2, the sixth state of consciousness was described as the experience of the finest level of changing values together with non-change; the finest level is represented by the horizontal line. Subjectively it is experienced as a growth of love and joy, and everything becomes more vivid, similar to the description from Jane Goodall quoted in Chapter 6. "Fortunate are those," writes Maharishi, "whose hearts flow in love."[4]

4. The growth of love culminates in Unity Consciousness where the changing values above the horizontal line are

appreciated in terms of the unboundedness of one's own Self shown below the line. This happens spontaneously after some time.

Katz describes the development of Transcendental Consciousness as follows: "We first locate it in the depths of meditation. Then we find it persisting even during daily life. Finally we see it as daily life."[5] For a fuller explanation I would recommend Katz's introduction to volume one of *Conversations with Maharishi*. The implication is that consciousness is the common basis to objectivity and subjectivity.

5.   Towards the end of Chapter 5 I made a brief reference to Brahman and defined it as incorporating both change and non-change, which would be represented by the whole of the chart. The silence of the Transcendent, and the dynamism within the Transcendent as a result of consciousness knowing itself, is the basis of all the surface change we see around us. Brahman can be thought of as an extension of unity consciousness:

In the beginning days of Unity only the first focus – the object of first attention – is in terms of the Self, and when this state is lived for a while the object of the second focus also participates in the same value. A little more practice, a little more living of Unity, and even the objects of the third-grade focus and the fourth-grade focus [are in terms of the Self]... the ability to appreciate the farther values of the Self keeps increasing...due to its different characteristic, [it] has been given a name: Brahman Consciousness.[6]

There is "acceptance of everything as the wholeness of my own unboundedness".[7] In his commentary on the Bhagavad Gita, Maharishi writes:

Brahman is that which cannot be expressed in words, even though the Upanishads use words to educate us about Its nature. In the field of speech, Brahman lies between two contrary statements...It is the eternal imperishable even while it is ever-changing. It is said to be both this and that. It is spoken of as Sat-Chit-Ananda [truth, consciousness, bliss] but includes what is not Sat, what is not Chit and what is not Ananda. It is beyond speech and thought, yet the whole range of thought and speech lie within it...Brahman is lived by man with ease but cannot be spoken of, in the sense that words are inadequate to encompass That which is the unlimited fullness of transcendental Being and the fullness of activity of life at the same time.[8]

The development of higher states of consciousness is the result of the natural growth of finer values of perception; it does not happen by thinking about them or making a mood or creating an intellectual construct. Just as the Yoga Sutras of Patanjali describe the path and goal of Yoga, so Brahman is described by the Brahma Sutras of Vyasa. Near the beginning of the Brahma Sutras, Brahman is described as, *That is harmony (synthesis),* which is why growth towards Brahman can heal social divisions. From the perspective of Brahman, consciousness is all there is and hence the famous Vedic expression: *I am that, you are that, all this is that.* Maharishi used an analogy of the sap that manifests as all parts of the tree, whether it is the fruit, flowers or branches:

The reality is the sap; flower, fruit and so on are just its phenomenal aspects. If we analyse the flower we see that every fibre of the petal is nothing but sap...And when it happens that the sap dominates the vision, and the leaf and this colour and all these distinctions, all these differences become overshadowed by the domination of the colourless quality of the sap, then Unity is said to be established in life...The leaf will be seen in terms of the sap.[9]

Should we be concerned with Lyotard's postmodernist warning at the start of Chapter 2 about grand narratives as Maharishi describes Brahman as total knowledge? This objection is answered by two academics from Maharishi International University:

> This total viewpoint is not "totalising" in the sense of making any one theory dominant but an actual experience from the all-inclusive foundation of consciousness. From this level, any individual contribution, any theory, can be appreciated and examined, not as an end itself, but for its evolutionary value. By placing all theory in this universal context, located within the student's own consciousness, the usefulness of all approaches can be honoured.[10]

A glimpse of a higher state of consciousness is described by Federico Faggin in his autobiography, *Silicon*. Faggin is the inventor of the microprocessor, and in 2010 President Obama presented Faggin with the National Medal of Technology and Innovation, the highest honour the United States confers for achievements related to technological progress. Having made his fortune with microprocessors, he began to work in the field of artificial intelligence and the development of touch pads and touch screens. For years he "tried to understand how consciousness could arise from electrical or biochemical signals".[11] Faggin, who studied physics at the University of Padua in Italy, says that up to the age of 40 he would have described himself as a materialist, having abandoned his childhood religious beliefs. He notes that if someone else had described the experience related below, he "would have dismissed it as their vivid imagination, as a daydream with no reality". Like Koestler in Chapter 2 he describes his experience as "a reality more real than the physical world I had previously thought was the only reality".[12]

Over Christmas 1990 he got up around midnight to get himself a drink of water while staying at Lake Tahoe, which is on the border of California and Nevada.

When I went back to bed and tried to fall asleep again, I felt a powerful rush of energy emerge from my chest like nothing I had ever felt before and could not even imagine possible. The feeling was love, but a love so intense and so incredibly fulfilling that it surpassed any other notions I had about love. Even more unbelievable was the fact that I knew I was the source of this love. I experienced it as a broad beam of shimmering white light, alive and beatific, gushing from my heart with incredible strength.

Then suddenly that light exploded. It filled the room and expanded to embrace the entire universe with the same white brilliance. I *knew* then, without a shadow of a doubt, that this was the substance from which all that exists is made. This was what created the universe out of itself. Then, with immense surprise, I *knew* that *I was that light!*

The entire experience lasted perhaps one minute, and it changed me forever. My relationship with the world had always been as a separate observer perceiving the universe as outside myself and disconnected from me. What made this event astonishing was its impossible perspective because I was *both* the experiencer *and* the experience. I was simultaneously the observer of the world and the world. I was the world observing itself! I was concurrently knowing that the world is made of a substance that feels like love, and that I *am* that substance!

In other words, the essence of reality was revealed to be a substance that knows itself in its self-reflection, and its self-knowing feels like an irrepressible and dynamic love.

This experience contained an unprecedented force of truth because it felt true at all the levels of my being. At the physical level, my body was alive and vibrant like I had never felt before. At the emotional level, I experienced myself as an impossibly powerful source of love, and at the mental level I knew with certainty that all is "made of love."

That experience also manifested the existence of another level of reality never previously lived: a spiritual level where I felt one with the world. This was *direct knowing*, stronger than the certainty that human logic provides; a knowing from the inside rather than from the outside involving for the first time the concurrence and resonance of all of my conscious aspects: the physical, emotional, mental, and spiritual.

I like to think that I experienced my nature both as a particle and as a wave, to use an analogy with quantum physics otherwise impossible to comprehend with the ordinary logical mind. The particle aspect was the ability to maintain my unique identity despite also being the world, which was the wave aspect. And yet, even my identity was part of the world, not me, because I experienced myself as the world rather than "my" point of view. Thus, I now see my identity as that unique point of view with which One – All that is, the totality of what exists – observes and knows itself. I am a point of view of One, a portion of One indivisible from it.

My experience has maintained its original intensity and clarity over the years and has changed my life from the inside out. It also continues to have a powerful impact to this day.[13]

Note that Faggin was not following any kind of spiritual path at the time of this experience; it was spontaneous and unexpected, but it is a perspective that Maharishi could endorse; the difference is that unity consciousness is when the non-Self is appreciated in terms of one's Self on a stable and permanent basis. *And in the end* healing social divisions depends on the unifying force of love. To quote Maharishi: "the silent force of love knows no barriers" and "no precious drop of love is ever wasted."[14]

About the author

Barry Spivack studied Philosophy, Politics and Economics at Oxford University before training as a teacher of Transcendental Meditation. For 25 years he combined working in industry with teaching Transcendental Meditation part-time. He currently teaches Transcendental Meditation in Essex, mainly in schools and companies, with patients in the UK's National Health Service and is due to start a project with the British Armed Forces. His previous book, *An Antidote to Violence: Evaluating the Evidence*, was co-authored with Dr Patricia Saunders and was Changemakers Books' best-selling book of 2020.

Barry can be contacted through the website healingsocialdivisions.org

References and notes

Introduction

1. Smith, D. & Gambino, L. (9 November 2020). Joe Biden gets to work as president-elect while Trump refuses to concede. *Guardian* newspaper.
2. Galtung, J. (2002). *Searching for peace: the road to TRANSCEND*. London, UK: Pluto Press, 126.
3. Spivack, B. & Saunders, P. (2020). *An antidote to violence: evaluating the evidence*. Hampshire, UK: Changemakers Books.

Chapter 1: Neutralizing social tensions

1. Putnam, R.D. (1993). *Making democracy work: civic traditions in modern Italy*. Princeton, NJ: Princeton University Press.
2. Durkheim, E. (1893/1989). *The division of labour in society*. London, UK: Macmillan Education, 65.
3. Smith, K. (2014). *Emile Durkheim and the collective consciousness of society: a study in criminology*. London, UK: Anthem Press, 155.
4. Ibid. 189.
5. Ibid.
6. Maharishi Mahesh Yogi. (1987). *Maharishi's programme to create world peace: demonstrating the mechanics to create coherence in world consciousness, the basis of world peace*. Vlodrop, Netherlands: MERU Press, 563.
7. Maharishi Mahesh Yogi. (1995). *Maharishi's absolute theory of government: automation in administration*. India: Age of Enlightenment Publications, 62.
8. Maharishi Mahesh Yogi. (1969). *On the Bhagavad-Gītā: a new translation and commentary with Sanskrit text*. London, UK: Penguin, 432.
9. Maharishi in B. Oates, (1976). *Celebrating the dawn: Maharishi*

Mahesh Yogi and the TM technique. New York, NY: G.P. Putnam's Sons, 37.

10. Travis, F. & Parim, N. (2017). Default mode network activation and Transcendental Meditation practice: focused attention or automatic self-transcending? *Brain and Cognition*, (111)92.

11. Maharishi in Oates, (1976), 75–6.

12. Maharishi, (1969), 12.

13. Chalmers, R. (16 July 2019). https://uk.tm.org/ documents/12132/17158243/TM+Research+Summary+2019/ dcd2170d-9555-47ee-b313-e182e31f84b1. Retrieved 13 December 2020.

14. Orme-Johnson, D.W. & Barnes, V.A. (2014). Effects of the transcendental meditation technique on trait anxiety: a meta-analysis of randomized controlled trials. *Journal of Alternative and Complementary Medicine*, (5)330–41. doi: 10.1089/acm.2013.0204. Epub 2013 Oct 9. PMID: 24107199. Eppley, K.R., Abrams, A.I. & Shear, J. (1989). Differential effects of relaxation techniques on trait anxiety: a meta-analysis. *Journal of Clinical Psychology*, (45)957–74.

15. Travis, F., Haaga, D.A., Hagelin, J., Tanner, M., Arenander, A., Nidich, S., Gaylord-King, C., Grosswald, S., Rainforth, M. & Schneider, R.H. (2010). A self-referential default brain state: patterns of coherence, power, and eLORETA sources during eyes-closed rest and Transcendental Meditation practice. *Cognitive Processing*, (1)21–30. doi: 10.1007/s10339-009-0343-2. Epub 2009 Oct 28. PMID: 19862565.

16. Dillbeck, M.C. & Bronson, E.C. (1981). Short-term longitudinal effects of the Transcendental Meditation technique on EEG power and coherence. *International Journal of Neuroscience*, (14)147–51. Gaylord, C., Orme-Johnson, D.W. & Travis, F. (1989). The effects of the Transcendental Meditation technique and progressive muscular relaxation on EEG coherence, stress

reactivity, and mental health in black adults. *International Journal of Neuroscience*, (46)77–86.

Travis, F. & Wallace, R.K. (1999). Autonomic and EEG patterns during eyes-closed rest and transcendental meditation (TM) practice: the basis for a neural model of TM practice. *Conscious Cognition*, 8(3)302–18.

Yam Yamamoto, Shin & Kitamura, Yoshihiro & Yamada, Norihito & Nakashima, Yoshihiko & Kuroda, Shigetoshi. (2006). Medial prefrontal cortex and anterior cingulate cortex in the generation of alpha activity induced by Transcendental Meditation: a magnetoencephalographic study. *Acta medica Okayama*, (60)51–8. doi: 10.18926/AMO/30752.

Travis, F. & Arenander, A. (2006). Cross-sectional and longitudinal study of effects of transcendental meditation practice on interhemispheric frontal asymmetry and frontal coherence. *International Journal of Neuroscience*, 116(12)1519–38. doi: 10.1080/00207450600575482. PMID: 17145686.

17. Travis, F. (2020). Temporal and spatial characteristics of meditation EEG. *Psychological Trauma: Theory, Research, Practice, and Policy*, 12(2)111–15. https://doi.org/10.1037/tra0000488.

18. Chalmers, (16 July 2019). References 12, 101, 175, 266, 270, 275, 276, 278, 283, 284, 296, 297, 310 , 311, 313, 314 and 315.

19. Travis, F., Haaga, D.A., Hagelin, J., Tanner, M., Nidich, S., Gaylord-King, C., Grosswald, S., Rainforth, M., Schneider R.H. (2009). Effects of Transcendental Meditation practice on brain functioning and stress reactivity in college students, *International Journal of Psychophysiology*, (71)2.

20. Nidich, S., Mills, J., Rainforth, M., Heppner, P., Schneider, R.H., Rosenthal, N.E., Salerno, J., Gaylord-King, C. & Rutledge, T. (2018). Non-trauma-focused meditation versus exposure therapy in veterans with post-traumatic stress disorder: a randomised controlled trial. *Lancet Psychiatry*,

5(12)975–86.

21. Maharishi Mahesh Yogi. (1979). *World Government News*, 11. Rheinweiler, Germany: Maharishi European Research University Press, 38.

Chapter 2: Beyond language and ideology

1. Cooke, M. (2006). *Re-presenting the good society*. Cambridge, MA: MIT Press.

2. The six systems are Nyaya, Vaisheshik, Samkhya, Yoga, Karma Mimamsa and Vedanta. The first three present the intellectual aspect and the last three present the experiential nature of the path to enlightenment. Maharishi does not regard these systems as competing but considers them as one integrated whole.

3. Maharishi, (1969), 470. See Chapter 1, note 8.

4. The claim that we are locked within specific language games or discourses is itself an absolute claim and so from a relativistic postmodernist standpoint a self-contradiction. Following Wittgenstein, language games represent a series of family resemblances.

5. Pearson, C.A. (2016). *The supreme awakening: experiences of enlightenment throughout time – and how you can cultivate them* (2nd ed.). Fairfield, IA: MUM Press, 168.

6. Maharishi, (1969), 314.

7. Dillbeck, M.C. (2020). Introduction in M.C. Dillbeck, et al. (eds), *Scientific research on Maharishi's Transcendental Meditation and TM-Sidhi program: collected papers, volume 8*. Switzerland: Maharishi European Research University Press, lxxxix.

8. Alexander, C.N., Davies, J.L., Dixon, C.A., Dillbeck, M.C., Druker, S.M., Oetzel, R.M., Muehlman, J.M. & Orme-Johnson, D.W. (1990). Growth of higher stages of consciousness: Maharishi's Vedic psychology of human development, in C.N. Alexander and E.J. Langer (eds), *Higher stages of*

human development: perspectives on adult growth beyond formal operations. Oxford, UK: Oxford University Press, 298.

9. Ibid.

10. Pearson, (2016), 148.

11. Hume, D. (1739/2003). *A Treatise of Human Nature* (I, iv, 6). Mineola, NY: Dover Philosophical Classics, 180.

12. Pearson, (2016), 176.

13. Maharishi, (1969), 396.

14. Travis, F. (1994). The junction point model: a field model of waking, sleeping, and dreaming relating dream witnessing, the waking/sleeping transition, and Transcendental Meditation in terms of a common psychophysiologic state. *Dreaming,* (4)91–104. doi: 10.1037/h0094404.

15. Pearson, (2016), 500.

16. Mason, L.L., Alexander, C.N., Travis, F.T., Marsh, G., Orme-Johnson, D.W., Gackenbach, J., Mason, D.C., Rainforth, M. & Walton, K.G. (1997). Electrophysiological correlates of higher states of consciousness during sleep in long-term practitioners of the Transcendental Meditation program. *Sleep,* (20)102–10.

17. Maharishi Mahesh Yogi. (1966). *The science of Being and the art of living.* Fairfield, IA: MIU Press, 113.

18. Maharishi in V. Katz, (2011). *Conversations with Maharishi: Maharishi Mahesh Yogi speaks about the full development of human consciousness.* Fairfield, IA: MUM Press, 30. Katz was born in Germany and emigrated to the UK at the age of 11 via the kindertransport. He completed his education at Oxford University where he gained a first class honours degree in Philosophy, Politics and Economics. One of his tutors was Harold Wilson, who had become an economics don at the university at the age of 21, one of the youngest in the last century, and went on to become Prime Minister of the UK, winning four elections. Katz's PhD was in Indian Philosophy, under the supervision of Sarvepalli

Radhakrishnan, a professor at Oxford and fellow of All Souls College who became the second president of India and was nominated for a Nobel Prize in Literature 16 times and for the Nobel Peace Prize 11 times. As outstanding as Wilson and Radhakrishnan were, in Katz's view, neither compared with the brilliance and originality of Maharishi.

19. Pearson, (2016), 315.

20. Maharishi, (1969), 358.

21. Katz, (2011), 44.

22. Alexander, C.N., Rainforth, M.V. & Gelderloos, P. (1991). Transcendental Meditation, self-actualization, and psychological health: a conceptual overview and statistical meta-analysis. *Journal of Social Behavior and Personality*, (6)189–247. The researchers explained how they selected all the papers: 'Through exhaustive hand and computer searches, we located all empirical studies on self-actualization and meditation or relaxation up to December 1990. Forty-two such articles and dissertations were located through computerized searches of *Psychological Abstracts*, *Science Citation Index*, *Dissertation Abstracts International* and *Sociological Abstracts* on the key words of *self-actualization* in conjunction with *meditation* and *relaxation*, as well as by bibliographic searches of review articles and collected TM research.'

23. Maslow, A.H. (1968). *Toward a psychology of being* (2nd ed.). New York, NY: Van Nostrand Reinhold, 26.

24. The 12 subscales on the personal orientation inventory are: time competence, inner directedness, self-actualizing values, existentiality, feeling reactivity, spontaneity, self-regard, self-acceptance, nature of man constructive, synergy, acceptance of aggression and capacity for intimate contact. The average length of each study was 12 weeks.

25. Ferguson, P.C. & Gowan, J.C. (1976). Psychological findings on Transcendental Meditation. *Journal of Humanistic*

Psychology, (16)51–60.

Chandler, H.M., Alexander C.N. & Heaton, D.P. (2005). Transcendental Meditation and postconventional self-development: a 10-year longitudinal study. *Journal of Social Behavior and Personality*, (17)93–122.

Nidich, S., O'Connor, T., Rutledge, T., Duncan, J., Compton, B., Seng, A. & Nidich, R. (2016). Reduced trauma symptoms and perceived stress in male prison inmates through the Transcendental Meditation Program: a randomized controlled trial. *Permanente Journal*, 20(4)43–7. All p values were <0.001. The Cohen effect sizes ranged from 0.67 to 0.89.

Nidich, S., Seng, A., Compton, B., O'Connor, T., Salerno, J.W. & Nidich, R. (2017). Transcendental Meditation and reduced trauma symptoms in female inmates: a randomized controlled study. *Permanente Journal*, 21. doi: 10.7812/TPP/16-008.

26. Orme-Johnson, (2014) and Eppley, (1989). See Chapter 1, note 14.

27. Pearson, (2016), 263.

28. Bancroft, A. (2000). *The Buddha speaks: a book of guidance from the Buddhist scriptures*. Boston, MA: Shambhala, 155.

29. Maharishi, (1969), 419.

30. The Maha Prajna Paramita Hrdaya Sutra. https://static1.squarespace.com/static/58d013bbe58c6272b30dad0b/t/59b04a9fd55b41f0f333b554/1504725663797/Heart-Sutra-in-English-text1.pdf. Retrieved 15 December 2020.

31. The Lamb shift, named after physicist Willis Lamb, is the most famous example. In 1955 he won the Nobel Prize in Physics for his discovery. https://en.wikipedia.org/wiki/Lamb_shift. Retrieved 15 December 2020.

32. Cooke, M. (2019). A pluralist model of democracy, in K. Volker & I. Salvatore (eds), *What is pluralism? The question of pluralism in politics*. London, UK: Routledge, 139–55.

33. Twenge, J.M. & Foster, J.D. (2010). Birth cohort increases in narcissistic personality traits among American college students, 1982–2009. *Social Psychological and Personality Science*, (1)99–106.

34. Taylor, C. (2018). *The ethics of authenticity*. Cambridge, MA: Harvard University Press, 39.

35. Alexander, C., Rainforth, M., Frank, P., Grant, J., Von Stade, C. & Walton, K. (2003). Walpole study of the Transcendental Meditation program in maximum security prisoners: III. Reduced recidivism. *Journal of Offender Rehabilitation*, (36)161–80.

36. Bleick, C.R. & Abrams, A.I. (1987). The Transcendental Meditation programme and criminal recidivism in California. *Journal of Criminal Justice*, (15)211–30.
    Rainforth, M.V., Alexander, C.N. & Cavanaugh, K.L. Effects of the Transcendental Meditation programme on recidivism among former inmates of Folsom Prison: survival analysis of 15-year follow-up data. *Journal of Offender Rehabilitation*, (36)181–203.

37. Anklesaria, F.K. & King, M.S. (2003). The Transcendental Meditation programme in the Senegalese penitentiary system. *Journal of Offender Rehabilitation*, 36(1–4)303–18. doi: 10.1300/j076v36n01_14.

38. Maharishi, (1966), 36–7.

39. Schecter, H. (1977). The Transcendental Meditation program in the classroom: a psychogical evaluation, in D.W. Orme-Johnson & J.T. Farrow (eds), *Scientific research on Maharishi's Transcendental Meditation and TM-Sidhi program: collected papers, volume 1*. Switzerland: Maharishi European Research University Press, 403–9.

40. Durkheim, (1893/1989), 24. See Chapter 1, note 2.

41. Benhabib, S. (2018). *Exile, statelessness, and migration: playing chess with history from Hannah Arendt to Isaiah Berlin*. Princeton, NJ: Princeton University Press, 171.

42. Maharishi, (1969), 156.

43. Ibid. 44.

44. Maharishi Mahesh Yogi. (1986). *Thirty years around the world: dawn of the Age of Enlightenment.* Vlodrop, Netherlands: MVU Press, 207.

45. Ibid. 208.

Chapter 3: Collective traumas and glories

1. Attributed to Maharishi Mahesh Yogi during an interview with an American journalist, according to J. Boncheff in his course *Maharishi's early years of teachings: 1965–1975.*

2. Volkan, V.D. (2020). *Large-group psychology: racism, societal divisions, narcissistic leaders and who we are now.* Bicester, UK: Phoenix, xiv.

3. Ibid. 19.

4. Ibid. 59.

5. Ibid. xiv.

6. Dillbeck, M.C. Research TM.Net. https://researchtm.net/search-form/ website health outcome. Retrieved 21 May 2021.

7. Rosenthal, N. (2011). *Transcendence: healing and transformation through Transcendental Meditation.* London, UK: Hay House, 73.

8. La Torre, G., Van Beeck, E., Quaranta, G., Mannocci, A. & Ricciardi, W. (2007). Determinants of within-country variation in traffic accident mortality in Italy: a geographical analysis. *International Journal of Health Geography,* (6)49. https://doi.org/10.1186/1476-072X-6-49.
Eckersley, R. & Dear, K. (2002). Cultural correlates of youth suicide. *Social Science and Medicine,* 55(11):1891–904. doi: 10.1016/s0277-9536(01)00319-7. PMID: 12406459.

9. Hagelin, J.S., Rainforth, M.V., Orme-Johnson, D.W., Cavanaugh, K.L., Alexander, C.N., Shatkin, S.F. et al. (1999). Effects of group practice of the Transcendental Meditation

program on preventing violent crime in Washington DC: results of the national demonstration project, June–July 1993. *Social Indicators Research*, 47(2)153–201.

10. Adapted from Fergusson, L. & Cavanaugh, K.L. (2019). Socio-political violence in Cambodia between 1990–2008: an explanatory mixed methods study of social coherence. *Journal of Maharishi Vedic Research Institute*, (10)43–126.

11. Steinberg, G.M. (2013). The limits of peacebuilding theory, in R. Mac Ginty (ed.), *Routledge Handbook of Peacebuilding*, Abingdon, UK: Routledge, 36.

12. Wallace, R.K. & Marcus, J.B. (2005). *Victory before war*. Fairfield, IA: Maharishi University of Management Press, inside front cover.

13. Nader, T.M., Alexander, C.N. & Davies, J.L. (1989). The Maharishi Technology of the Unified Field and reduction of armed conflict: a comparative, longitudinal study of Lebanese villages, in R.A. Chalmers, G. Clements, H. Schenkluhn & M. Weinless (eds), *Scientific research on Maharishi's Transcendental Meditation and TM-Sidhi program: collected papers, volume 4*. Vlodrop, Netherlands: Maharishi Vedic University Press, 2623–4.

14. Orme-Johnson, D.W., Alexander, C.N., Davies, J.L., Chandler, H.M. & Larimore, W.E. (1988). International peace project in the Middle East: the effect of the Maharishi Technology of the Unified Field. *Journal of Conflict Resolution*, 32(4)776–812.

15. Alexander-Herriot, V. (2012). Management and law: the legal environment of business, in D. Llewellyn (ed.), *Consciousness is primary: illuminating the leading edge of knowledge: proceedings of the 2012 faculty symposium at MUM with Professor Tony Nader*. Fairfield, IA: MUM Press, 266.

16. Orme-Johnson, D.W. & Oates, R.M. (2009). A field-theoretic view of consciousness: reply to critics. *Journal of Scientific Exploration*, 22(3)139–66.

17. Brown, C.L. (1996). Observing the assessment of research information by peer reviewers, newspaper reporters, and potential governmental and non-governmental users: International Peace Project in the Middle East (unpublished doctoral dissertation). Cambridge, MA: Harvard University, 87.

18. Orme-Johnson & Oates, (2009).

19. Russet, B. (1988). Editor's comment. *Journal of Conflict Resolution*, 32(4)773.

20. Ibid.

21. Fergusson, L., & Cavanaugh, K.L. (2019). (10)43–126. See note 10 above.

22. Maharishi Mahesh Yogi & Golan, M. (1976). *Matti Golan interviews Maharishi*. https://www.youtube.com/watch?v=8dBhACouXj4&t=1863s. Retrieved 3 March 2021.

23. Both an enemy and a criminal wish to cause harm.

24. Davies, J.L. & Alexander C.N. (2005). Alleviating political violence through reducing collective tension: impact assessment analysis of the Lebanon war. *Journal of Social Behavior and Personality*, (17)285–338.

25. Davies, J.L. (1992). Assessing the impact of coherence-creating groups on the Lebanon war. *Modern Science and Vedic Science* 5(1–2)145.

26. Davies & Alexander, (2005), 315–16.

27. Ibid. 328.

28. Pearson, C. (2008). *The complete book of Yogic Flying*. Fairfield, IA: MUM Press, 299.

29. Killelea, S. (2020). *Peace in the age of chaos: the best solution for a sustainable future*. Melbourne, Australia: Hardie Grant Books, 243.

30. Brown, (1996), 69.

31 Orme-Johnson, D.W. *Truth about TM*. https://www.truthabouttm.org/SocietalEffects/Critics-Rebuttals/. Retrieved 11 May 2021.

32. The probability of the result occurring by chance was less than one in ten million trillion, $p=9\times10^{20}$. See note 24 above, 322. Effect sizes of up to f>.59 were found with some of the variables measured in the studies in note 34.

33. Cavanaugh, K. (26 August 2021), personal communication.

34. Dillbeck, M.C. & Cavanaugh, K.L. (2016). Societal violence and collective consciousness: reduction of U.S. homicide and urban violent crime rates. *SAGE Open*, 6(2)1–16. http://sgo.sagepub.com/content/6/2/2158244016637891.

Cavanaugh, K.L. & Dillbeck, M.C. (2017). Field effects of consciousness and reduction in U.S. urban murder rates: evaluation of a prospective quasi-experiment. *Journal of Health and Environmental Research*, 3(3–1)34.

Cavanaugh, K.L. & Dillbeck, M.C. (2017). The contribution of proposed field effects of consciousness to the prevention of US accidental fatalities: theory and empirical tests. *Journal of Consciousness Studies*, 24(1–2)53–86.

Dillbeck, M.C. & Cavanaugh, K.L. (2017). Group practice of the Transcendental Meditation and TM-Sidhi program and reductions in infant mortality and drug-related death: a quasi-experimental analysis. *SAGE Open*, 7(1)1–15. https://doi.org/10.1177/2158244017697164.

35. Orme-Johnson, D.W., Cavanaugh, K.L. & Dillbeck, M.C. (2020). Field effects of consciousness: the influence of group practice of the Transcendental Medtiation and TM-Sidhi programme on the US quality of life, 2000–2016, in preparation.

36. McKnight, C. Quoted in B. Spivack & P.A. Saunders. (2020). *An antidote to violence: evaluating the evidence*. Hampshire, UK: Changemakers Books, opening testimonial.

Chapter 4: Varieties of freedom

1. Maharishi Mahesh Yogi, (1969), 209. See Chapter 1, note 8.
2. Ibid. 17.

3. Oliver, T. (2020). *The self delusion: the surprising science of how we are connected and why that matters.* London, UK: Weidenfeld & Nicholson, 162.

4. Hawkins, M. (2003). Effectiveness of the Transcendental Meditation programme in criminal rehabilitation and substance abuse recovery: a review of the research. *Journal of Offender Rehabilitation,* (36)47–65.

5. Maharishi, (1976), in Oates, 123. See Chapter 1, note 9.

6. Zmigrod, L., Rentfrow, P.J. & Robbins, T.W. (2020). The partisan mind: is extreme political partisanship related to cognitive inflexibility? *Journal of Experimental Psychology: General,* 149(3)407–18. https://doi.org/10.1037/xge0000661. https://www.cam.ac.uk/research/news/mental-rigidity-at-the-root-of-intense-political-partisanship-on-both-left-and-right-study. Retrieved 29 December 2020.

7. Pelletier, K.R. (1974). Influence of Transcendental Meditation upon autokinetic perception. *Perceptual and Motor Skills* (39)1031–4.

   Jedrczak, A. (1984). The Transcendental Meditation and TM-Sidhi program and field independence. *Perceptual and Motor Skills,* (59)999–1000.

   Fergusson, L.C. (1993). Field independence, transcendental meditation, and achievement in college art: a reexamination. *Perceptual and Motor Skills,* 77(3 Pt. 2):1104-6. doi: 10.2466/pms.1993.77.3f.1104. PMID: 8170755.

8. Mill, J.S. (1990). *Utilitarianism.* Glasgow, UK: William Collins, 135.

9. Walton, K.G. & Levitsky, D.K. (2003). Effects of the Transcendental Meditation program on neuroendocrine abnormalities associated with aggression and crime. *Journal of Offender Rehabilitation,* (36)67–87.

10. Walton, K., Pugh, N.D.C. & Cavanaugh, K.L. (2005). Effect of group practice of the Transcendental Meditation programme on biochemical indicators of stress in non-

meditators: a prospective time series analysis. *Journal of Social Behaviour and Personality*, (17)339–73.

The researchers used a test for 'Granger-causality'. The number of time lags was determined by minimization of the Bayesian Information Criterion. The Phillips-Perron test was used to examine for evidence of stationarity which was complemented by the Newey-West method. Other tests included the Breusch-Godfrey test, split-sample test, the predictive failure test and the Jarque-Bera test.

Pugh, N.D.C., Walton, K.G. & Cavanaugh, K.L. (1988). Can time series analysis of serotonin turnover test the theory that consciousness is a field? *Society of Neuroscience Abstracts*, (14)372.

Löliger, S.A. (1990). Relationship between subjective bliss, 5-hydroxy-3-in doleacetic acid and the collective practice of Maharishi's TM and TM-Sidhi program (unpublished doctoral dissertation). Fairfield, IA: Maharishi University of Management.

11. Eren, O. & Mocan, N. (2018). Emotional judges and unlucky juveniles. *American Economic Journal: Applied Economics*, 10(3)171–205.

12. So, K.T. & Orme-Johnson, D.W. (2001). Three randomized experiments on the longitudinal effects of the Transcendental Meditation technique on cognition. *Intelligence*, 29(5)419–40.

13. Rosenthal, N. (2016). *Super mind: how to boost performance and live a richer and happier life through Transcendental Meditation.* New York, NY: Tarcher/Penguin, 94.

14. Travis, F. (1979). The Transcendental Meditation technique and creativity: a longitudinal study of Cornell University undergraduates. *Journal of Creative Behavior*, 13(3)169–80. https://doi.org/10.1002/j.2162-6057.1979.tb00203.x.

15. Ní Shúilleabháin, A. (2016). The Irish man who discovered quaternion algebra. *Irish Times*. https://www.irishtimes.

com/news/science/the-irish-man-who-discovered-quaternion-algebra-1.2833168. Retrieved 3 March 2021.

16. Taylor, C.L. (2017). Creativity and mood disorder: a systematic review and meta-analysis. *Perspectives on Psychological Science*, 12(6)1040–76.

17. Bonshek, A. (2001). *Mirror of consciousness: art, creativity and Veda*. Delhi, India: Motilal Banarsidass, 295–9.

18. Hatchard, G. & Cavanaugh, K.L. (2017). The effect of coherent collective consciousness on national quality of life and economic performance indicators – an analysis of the IMD index of national competitive advantage. *Journal of Health and Environmental Research*. Special Issue: *Maharishi Vedic Science: Creating a Sustainable Future*, 3(3–1)16–31. doi: 10.11648/j.jher.s.2017030301.12.

19. Kohn, J. (2001). *The world of Hannah Arendt*. Library of Congress. https://www.loc.gov/loc/lcib/0103/arendt.html. Retrieved 8 March 2021.

20. Kattago, S. (2013). Why the world matters: Hannah Arendt's philosophy of new beginnings. *The European Legacy: Toward New Paradigms*, 18(2)170–184. doi: 10.1080/10848770.2013.772362.

21. Dai, T. (2011). Maharishi's formula for a prevention wing in the military – applied and found successful in Mozambique: case study 1993–1994, in R.S. Goodman & W.F. Sands (eds), *Consciousness-based education and government*. Fairfield, IA: Maharishi University of Management Press, 450.

22. Carbone, G.M. (2003). Emerging pluralist politics in Mozambique: the Frelimo-Renamo party system. *Crisis States Programme: Working papers series no. 1*. https://www.lse.ac.uk/international-development/Assets/Documents/PDFs/csrc-working-papers-phase-one/wp23-emerging-pluralist-politics-in-mozambique.pdf. Retrieved 3 March 2021.

23. Ibid.

24. Orre, A. & Ronning, H. (2017). Mozambique: a political economy analysis. *Norwegian Institute of International Affairs.* https://www.cmi.no/publications/file/6366-mozambique-a-political-economy-analysis.pdf. Retrieved 26 March 2021.

25. Fergusson, L. (2016). The impact of Maharishi Vedic University on Cambodian economic and social indicators from 1980 to 2015. *Journal of Maharishi Vedic Research Institute,* (2)77–135.

    Fergusson, L. (2016). Vedic science-based education, poverty removal and social well-being: a case history of Cambodia from 1980 to 2015. *Journal of Indian Education,* 41(4)16–45.

26. Hatchard, G. & Cavanaugh, K.L. (2009). The peace and well being of nations: An analysis of improved quality of life and enhanced economic performance through the Maharishi Effect in New Zealand, Norway, USA, Cambodia, and Mozambique—A longitudinal, cross-country, panel-regression analysis of the IMD Index of National Competitive Advantage. Hamilton, Ontario, Canada: Canadian Centers for Teaching Peace.

Chapter 5: The natural tendency of life

1. Parekh, B. Quoted in K. Smith, 203. See Chapter 1, note 3.
2. Maharishi, (1969), 118. See Chapter 1, note 8.
3. Rosenthal, (2016), 3. See Chapter 4, note 12.
4. In Pearson, C. (2008). *The complete book of Yogic Flying: Maharish Mahesh Yogi's programme for enlightenment and invincibility.* Fairfield, IA: MUM Press, 43.
5. Ibid. 47.
6. Maharishi, (1969), 437–8.
7. Pearson, (2016), 222. See Chapter 2, note 5.
8. Ibid. 209.
9. Ibid. 122.
10. Maharishi, (1969), 424.
11. Maharishi does not regard the Vedic literature as

philosophical treatises; rather they are the impulses of self-referral consciousness. In the dynamic process of knowing itself, consciousness self-generates the continuous Unmanifest Sound of self-referral consciousness. This is experienced as a self-referral hum but a hum where the gaps between the syllables are as important as any sound; silence and dynamism together. Recitation of Veda should ideally be from a profound, clear and less stressed level of consciousness; it would then be performative in the sense that it has a real influence on the world around us. Dr Tony Nader, medical doctor, physiologist and the head of the international Transcendental Meditation organization, has compared these sounds and gaps with the neurons and the synaptic gaps in the human physiology and discovered a striking parallel between the structure and function of the human nervous system and the Vedic Literature. Maharishi explains that Veda is not a composition, but rather it is the self-interacting rhythm of the Veda that is at the basis of orderliness that we see in nature. The Vedic Literature, according to Maharishi, is due to the continuing interactions between dynamism and silence; Maharishi describes it as the collapse of silence into dynamism, and dynamism into silence, and these interactions can in principle be heard. Maharishi describes this as a whirlpool; as when the flow of a river (remember Koestler's experience recounted in Chapter 2) is restricted, a whirlpool is created. In his book *Constitution of India*, Maharishi explains on page 20 that a whirlpool 'has dynamism at the surface and concentrated dynamism [silence] at its point'. Maharishi describes this interaction of the opposite values of silence and dynamism as the constitution of the universe, the home of all the laws of nature.

12. Katz, V. (2015). *The Upanishads: a new translation*. New York, NY: Tarcher/Penguin, 129.

13. Maharishi, (1966), 80. See Chapter 2, note 18.

Chapter 6: Unity and diversity

1. Pearson, (2016), 346. See Chapter 2, note 5.
2. Maharishi, (1969), 444. See Chapter 1, note 8.
3. Ibid. 50–2.
4. Eppley, (1989) and Orme-Johnson & Barnes, (2014). See Chapter 1, note 14.
5. https://researchtm.net/ Scientific research on Transcendental Meditation: collected papers, volumes 1–8. Retrieved 22 February 2021.
6. Iyer, V.R.K. (1977). First world assembly on law, justice and rehabilitation. Rheinweiler, Germany: MERU Press, 14.
7. Ibid. 32.
8. Ibid. 23.
9. Maharishi Mahesh Yogi. (1985). Inaugural address of His Holiness Maharishi Mahesh Yogi in Maharishi Mahesh Yogi: Maharishi Vedic University Inauguration. Washington DC, 65–6.
10. Ibid. 66.
11. Maharishi, (1969), 63.

Chapter 7: Coherence in collective consciousness: the ground for good governance

1. Maharishi in Oates, (1976), 96. See Chapter 1, note 9.
2. Putnam, (1993). See Chapter 1, note 1.
3. Mungiu-Pippidi, A. & Johnson, M. (2017). *Transitions to good governance: creating virtuous circles of anti-corruption.* Cheltenham, UK: Edward Elgar Publishing, 256.
4. Ibid. 4.
5. Ibid. 261–2.
6. Maharishi Mahesh Yogi. (1978). *Enlightenment to every individual: invincibility to every nation.* Rheinweiler, Germany: MERU Press, 247–8.

7. Ellis, G. (2012). *A symphony of silence: an enlightened vision.* North Charleston, SC: Create Space, 307.

8. Maharishi, (1966), 228. See Chapter 2, note 18.

9. Orrell, D. (2018). Why we missed the storm. *World finance: the voice of the market.* https://www.worldfinance.com/ banking/why-we-missed-the-storm. Retrieved 1 April 2021.

10. Akerlof, G.A. & Shiller, R.J. (2009). *Animal spirits: how human psychology drives the economy, and why it matters for global capitalism.* Princeton, NJ: Princeton University Press, 1.

11. Edmans, A., Fernandez-Perez, A., Garel, A. & Indriawan, I. (2021). Music sentiment and stock returns around the world. *Journal of Financial Economics*, forthcoming. Available at *SSRN*, https://ssrn.com/abstract=3776071 or http://dx.doi. org/10.2139/ssrn.3776071

12. Maharishi, (1995), 64. See Chapter 1, note 7.

13. Ibid. 61–3.

14. Brown, G. (2021). *Seven ways to change the world: how to fix the most pressing problems we face.* London, UK: Simon & Schuster, 108.

15. Chandhoke, N. (2019). *Rethinking pluralism, secularism and tolerance.* Dehli, India: Sage, 181. Commenting on Socrates' statement that he knew that he knew nothing, Chandhoke writes: "that all of us suffer from an epistemological deficit and that our knowledge is necessarily incomplete."

16. Rousseau, Jean-Jacques (2011). *Rousseau: the basic political writings: Discourse on the Sciences and the Arts, Discourse on the Origin of Inequality, Discourse on Political Economy, On the Social Contract, The State of War* (2nd ed.). Trans. D.A. Cress. Indianapolis, IA: Hackett, 167.

17. Maharishi quoted in A. Bonshek, (2001), 297. See Chapter 4, note 16.

18. Katz, V., (2011), 71. See Chapter 2, note 19.

19. Ibid. 70.

20. Maharishi, (1978), 319.
21. Gentile, V. (2013). *From identity-conflict to civil society: restoring human dignity and pluralism in deeply divided societies.* Rome, Italy: LUISS University Press.

    Gentile, V. (2018). From a culture of civility to deliberative reconciliation in deeply divided societies. *Journal of Social Philosophy,* 49(2)229–251.
22. British political theorist Isaiah Berlin (1909–97) maintained that there can be an inescapable clash of fundamental values which cannot be reconciled into a harmonious whole, as much as we may wish for that outcome. Berlin describes the desire for unity as a primitive and child-like craving for certainty. History has shown that well-intentioned attempts to enforce a vision of positive liberty may result in totalitarianism. Maharishi maintains that increasing unity from the transcendental level of life strengthens cultural diversity on the surface of life. Thus Maharishi and Berlin are approaching this from different perspectives and they are both correct from their own angle. Berlin is talking about the everyday changing world around us where we attempt to take control on the surface of events; Maharishi is talking about unity on the transcendental level of life which nourishes the surface. If a plant is starved of water then it will go a uniform brown as it dies. Putting water on the leaf or the flower will not help. If one waters the root then all the diverse aspects of the plant will flourish: the leaves, the branches, the flowers and any fruit it may produce. A favourite aphorism of Maharishi was *water the root to enjoy the fruit.* Increasing unity in the midst of diversity is the basis of healing social divisions but without sacrificing the richness of cultural variety. Moreover, Maharishi regards national traditions as maintaining stability, and if they are eroded, 'it is like a leaf at the mercy of the wind, blown in any direction, without stability or basis of its own' (*The*

Science of Being, 232). Maharishi is not imposing a doctrine on the surface of life but suggesting how human potential can be unfolded through an experience of restful alertness; it has its basis in human physiology, not intellectual reasoning. Maharishi and Berlin both agree that humans are choice-making creatures and those decisions are made within a context such as their culture, upbringing and so on. Maharishi is clear that people have to freely choose to meditate and they cannot be forced but rather should be inspired to take up the practice. Berlin advocates that minimizing suffering is the best goal a government can aim for and this has been Maharishi's motivation in promoting his various programmes, which have been supported by peer-reviewed scientific research. One can view Maharishi's programmes from either of two angles: reducing suffering or developing a person's full potential which has an effect on the well-being of society both nationally and globally. In his essay *Two Concepts of Liberty* Berlin summarizes a potential slippery slope from good intentions to totalitarianism as follows: 1. we have one true purpose of rational self-direction; 2. we all fit into a harmonious rational whole which some may be able to discern better than others; 3. all suffering is due to the lower irrational part of ourselves not being in tune with the higher rational part of our self; 4. those who know the truth, which could be a religious or political institution, exercise choice on our behalf. While Maharishi says that it is natural to evolve and gain higher states of consciousness so that we develop our full potential; that we fit into a whole that some can see more clearly than others; and that human suffering is due to a lack of knowledge of our higher Self; it does not follow that people should be forced to meditate. Given that Transcendental Meditation's efficacy depends on it being effortless, forcing a person to meditate would be self-defeating. We have to make the choice ourselves to seek Self-realization. Moreover, only a fraction of a population is needed to have an influence on society.

23. *Global Peace Initiative.* http://globalpeaceproject.net/proven-results/endorsements/. Retrieved 11 May 2021.

Chapter 8: A paradigm of connectivity

1. Lazar, S.W., Kerr, C.E., Wasserman, R.H., Gray, J.R., Greve, D.N., Treadway, M.T., McGarvey, M., Quinn, B.T., Dusek, J.A., Benson, H., Rauch, S.L., Moore, C.I. & Fischl, B. (2005). Meditation experience is associated with increased cortical thickness. *Neuroreport*, 16(17), 1893–7. https://doi.org/10.1097/01.wnr.0000186598.66243.19.

2. Mason, L., Peters, E., Williams, S. & Kumari., V. (2017). Brain connectivity changes occurring following cognitive behavioural therapy for psychosis predict long-term recovery. *Translational Psychiatry* (7)e1001. https://doi.org/10.1038/tp.2016.263.

3. Harvard Medical School. (2019). *The power of the placebo effect*. Harvard Health Publishing. https://www.health.harvard.edu/mental-health/the-power-of-the-placebo-effect. Retrieved 13 February 2021.
Marchant, J. (2017). *Cure: a journey in the science of mind over body*. Edinburgh, UK: Canongate Books.

4. Scientific and Medical Network, for example.

5. Eddington, A. (1974). The nature of the physical world. Chicago, IL: University of Michigan Press, 276.

6. Penrose, R., Shimony, A., Cartwright, N. & Hawking, S. (1997). The large, the small and the human mind. Cambridge, UK: Cambridge University Press, 181.

7. Schrödinger, E. (1967). *What is Life? and Mind and Matter*. Cambridge, UK: Cambridge University Press, 130.

8. Other physicists and mathematicians include three Nobel Laureates, Planck, Wigner and Josephson, then

also Whitehead, London, Bauer, Bohm, Hiley, Dyson, Wheeler, D'Espagnat, Sudarshan, Goswami, Carr, Hagelin, Stapp, Vitiello, Pessa, Alfinito, Beck, Fisher, Khrennikov, Atmanspacher, Filk, Kafatos, Roemer, de Gosson, Bruza, Haven, Radin.

9. Jedlicka, P. (2017). Revisiting the quantum brain hypothesis: toward quantum (neuro)biology? *Frontiers in Molecular Neuroscience*, (10)366. https://doi.org/10.3389/fnmol.2017.00366.

10. Maharishi Mahesh Yogi. (1977). *Creating an ideal society: a global undertaking*. Rheinweiler, Germany: MERU Press, 77.

11. Ibid. 79.

12. Ibid. 79–80.

13. Ibid. 85.

14. Pearson, (2016), 399. See Chapter 2, note 5.

15. Batchelor, M. (2000). Ten ox-herding pictures. *Tricycle*. https://tricycle.org/magazine/ten-oxherding-pictures/. Retrieved 11 May 2021.

16. Brown, (1996), 63. See Chapter 3, note 17.

Chapter 9: How to love your neighbour and your environment as yourself

1. Biden, J. (2021). *'Defend the truth and defeat the lies': Biden moves past Trump's war on media*, quoted by D. Folkenflik in NPR. https://www.npr.org/sections/inauguration-day-live-updates/2021/01/20/958523644/defend-the-truth-and-defeat-the-lies-biden-moves-past-trumps-war-on-media. Retrieved 17 February 2021.

2. Janezic, K.A. & Gallego, A. (2020). Eliciting preferences for truth-telling in a survey of politicians. *Proceedings of the National Academy of Sciences*. 117(36)22002–22008; doi: 10.1073/pnas.2008144117.

3. Arendt, H. (1977). Truth and politics, in *Between past and future*. London, UK: Penguin, 254.

4. Tsipursky, G. & Ward T. (2020). *Pro Truth: a practical plan to put truth back into politics.* Washington DC: Changemakers Books, 32.

5. Nidich, S., Ryncarz, R., Abrams, A., Orme-Johnson, D.W. & Wallace, R.K. (1983). Kohlbergian cosmic perspective responses, EEG coherence, and the TM and TM-Sidhi programme. *Journal of Moral Education,* 12 (3)166–73.

Kotchabhakdi, N.J., Pipatveravat, S., Kotchabhakdi, N., Tapanya, P. & Pornpathkul, S. (1982). Improvement of intelligence, learning ability and moral judgment through the practice of the Transcendental Meditation technique, in *Proceedings of the Second Asian Workshop on Child and Adolescent Development,* Bangkok and Bangsaen, Thailand, 15–24 February. Bangkok: Sri Nakharinwirot University.

Nidich, R.J., Nidich, S. I. & Alexander, C.N. (2005). Moral development and natural law. *Journal of Social Behaviour and Personality,* (17)137–49.

6. Maharishi, (1978), 137. See Chapter 7, note 6.

7. Maharishi, (1966), 103. See Chapter 2, note 18.

8. Maharishi, (1978), 183–5. When Maharishi uses the term natural law, he is translating the Sanskrit term dharma which has no direct equivalent in English. Here are some explanations about dharma taken from Maharishi's commentary on the first verse of the Bhagavad Gita: "'Dharma' is that invincible power of nature which upholds existence. It maintains evolution and forms the very basis of cosmic life. It supports all that is helpful for evolution and discourages all that is opposed to it...When the good increases in life and the positive forces tend to overbalance the normal state of existence, then the process of dharma, restoring equilibrium, results in feelings of happiness in the heart and satisfaction in the mind. In the same way, when evil increases in life and the negative forces predominate, the power of dharma, restoring the balance, produces sensations of pain and suffering...Assisting the

growth of negative forces results in suffering; when we help the positive forces to increase we share the joy of life. 'As you sow so shall you reap', expresses the role of dharma in practical life...Calamities, crises and catastrophes in a community or country are caused by the increase of negative forces resulting from the evil deeds of a majority of their people...Our individual life moves backwards and forwards automatically as we direct it under the influence of dharma. Positive and negative forces, as we develop them, play their role on the field of dharma and shape the destiny of life."

9. Skrbina, D. (2017). *Panpsychism in the West* (rev. ed.). Cambridge, MA: MIT Press, 313.

10. Wallace, R.K. & Marcus, J.B. (2005), inside front cover. See Chapter 3, note 12.

Appendix: Knowledge is different in different states of consciousness

1. Maharishi, (1966), 34. See Chapter 2, note 18.

2. Ibid. 34–5.

3. Ibid. 52.

4. Maharishi Mahesh Yogi. (1965). *Love and God.* Norway, Oslo: SRM, 15.

5. Maharishi in V. Katz, (2011), 43. See Chapter 2, note 19.

6. Ibid. 50–1.

7. Ibid. 53.

8 . Maharishi, (1969), 440–1. See Chapter 1, note 8.

9. Maharishi in Katz, 244–9.

10. Seltzer, S. & Fairchild, T. (1997). Consciousness and literary studies. *Modern Science and Vedic Science,* 7(1)127.

11. Faggin, F. (2021). *Silicon.* Cardiff, CA: Waterside Productions, 155.

12. Ibid. 161.

13. Ibid. 160–1.

14. Maharishi, (1965), 16 and 18 respectively.

Index

Also by the Author

An Antidote to Violence
Evaluating the Evidence
Barry Spivack and Dr. Patricia Saunders
Weaving together psychology, sociology, philosophy, statistics,
politics, physics and meditation An Antidote to Violence
provides evidence that we have the knowledge to reduce all
kinds of violence in society.
Paperback 978-1-78904-258-0; e-book: 978-1-78904-259-7

CHANGEMAKERS
BOOKS

TRANSFORMATION

Transform your life, transform your world - Changemakers Books publishes books for individuals committed to transforming their lives and transforming the world. Our readers seek to become positive, powerful agents of change. Changemakers Books inform, inspire, and provide practical wisdom and skills to empower us to write the next chapter of humanity's future.

Zombies on Kilimanjaro
A Father/Son Journey Above the Clouds
Tim Ward
On a journey to the roof of Africa, a father and son traverse the treacherous terrain of fatherhood, divorce, dark secrets and old grudges, and forge an authentic new relationship.
Paperback 978-1-78099-339-3; e-book: 978-1-78099-340-9

How to Lead a Badass Business From Your Heart
The Permission You've Been Waiting for to Birth Your Vision and Spread Your Glitter in the World
Makenzie Marzluff
A blueprint for conscious young entrepreneurs to bring their business to life in a way that is entirely rooted in the heart. While the old paradigm of business was rooted in fear and greed, this book grants full permission to visionaries to restore heart on our planet through their creations.
Paperback 978-1-78904-636-6; e-book: 978-1-78904-637-3

Everything You Never Learned About Sex
Take Back Your Masculine Power & Use Your Sex Energy For Good
Michael McPherson
Michael McPherson shines a light on what it was like for the men of his millennial generation to mature sexually, and why so many still haven't.
Paperback 978-1-78904-638-0; e-book 978-1-78904-639-7

Resilience **Series**

The Resilience Series is a collaborative effort by the authors of Changemakers Books in response to the 2020-21 coronavirus epidemic. Each concise volume offers expert advice and practical exercises for mastering specific skills and abilities. Our intention is that by strengthening your resilience, you can better survive and even thrive in a time of crisis.

www.resilience-books.com

Resetting Our Future **Series**

At this critical moment of history, with a pandemic raging, we have the rare opportunity for a Great Reset – to choose a different future. This series provides a platform for pragmatic thought leaders to share their vision for change based on their deep expertise. For communities and nations struggling to cope with the crisis, these books will provide a burst of hope and energy to help us take the first difficult steps towards a better future.

www.resettingourfuture.com